STANDING THROUGH THE STORM

Chad Robertson
Standing Through the Storm

Published by Spines
ISBN: 979-8-89691-128-9

STANDING THROUGH THE STORM

CHAD ROBERTSON

CONTENTS

I want to express my heartfelt gratitude to my mother and father for their unwavering support in my upbringing.

To my beloved current wife, Myrtle Robertson, my heart brims with love beyond what mere words can convey.

Irieonna, my precious daughter, you are the most beautiful blessing life has bestowed upon me.

A special mention to my grandmother, whose lessons in discipline have shaped my character.

I am also thankful to Pastor Chris Williams and his family for their kindness and the Pentecostals of Youngsville Church for the immense love they have shown my own family.

A nod of appreciation goes to Elder Edward Charles for his invaluable mentorship.

Finally, to all my wonderful family and friends who enrich my life, thank you from the depths of my heart. Remember, Jesus loves you all.

PROLOGUE

Why do you persist in your heedless chatter near me as if the weight of your words carried no consequence? I stand as the Alpha and the Omega, the beginning and the end, the embodiment of the divine plan that weaves through the tapestry of existence. I am acutely aware of your journey and your testimony—a narrative that is not meant for the masses but rather for the chosen nations, selected with purpose and profound intent. Your mission is a sacred whisper meant to resonate in the hearts of a few, igniting a flame that will ripen into a transformative force. Remember the wisdom of Matthew 4:19, spoken from ages past:

> “Follow me, and I will make you fishers of men."

Embrace this calling, for it is through your unique path that the spirit communes with the world.

It was noon, and I found myself wrestling once more with Leviathan, that malevolent serpent nestled deep within the ancient texts, a creature who, for far too long, had coiled around my spirit, suffocating my joy. This day, it constricted tighter, casting me down to the ground, a battle that felt both eternal and crushing. "Dad, where are you?" I whispered hopelessly, the void of his absence echoing louder than the serpent's taunts. The question hung heavily in the air, and I pondered, "Is this truly the day that the Lord has made?" If so, why did I feel so diminished, fading as if my very essence was seeping away like water through fingers in my early twenties?

"End it all," Leviathan hissed, its voice a slithering vine around my thoughts. But deep within, a stubborn ember flickered alive, urging me to rise, to step outside. "In the name of Jesus!" I roared, channeling the raw strength of a lion prowling through the vast and untamed African jungle. "Hear me, you seductive spirit! Depart from my life!" I commanded, defiance igniting my voice against the suffocating cloak of despair. At that moment, the world erupted in brilliance; colors exploded around me as if I were seeing the vibrant hues of life for the first time since I was fifteen. This day would be etched into my memory forever.

Compelled by a newfound resolve, I stepped into the sunlight and knelt in prayer, surrendering everything for the first time. It was an act of faith, a call into the profound silence of the universe, and then as if the heavens leaned down to listen—He answered. I could feel His presence enveloping me, a comforting strength seeping into my bones, promising to reveal to me what it truly meant to stand firm against the raging storms of life. It was a promise, unwavering and profound that this battle was not mine to fight alone.

CHAPTER ONE
UNYIELDING SPIRIT

> Before I formed thee in the belly, I knew thee; and before thou camest forth out of the womb, I sanctified thee, and I ordained thee a prophet unto the nations."
>
> JEREMIAH 1:5

To me, Mom was a precious gem, her life a testimony to resilience. It was during the dawn of my existence that she received a divine message: "You are nurturing a prophet in your womb." Judy Robertson was the epitome of grace and tidiness, a radiant soul whose presence brought joy to all. I can only imagine the moments she battled doubt, yet she held firm to the truth that "with God, all things are possible."

> "With men, this is impossible, but with God, all things are possible."
>
> MATTHEW 19:26

The day I grasped the significance of being called a king, she knelt beside me, her cheeks aglow, and said, "Chaddy, you're a king." Each morning, I eagerly awaited her voice—it was my anchor. Her culinary magic turned ordinary meals into feasts, fulfilling her dream of one day owning a daycare. In 1993, she opened Kids World Christian Child Care Center, a sanctuary where childhood thrived. "Mrs. Judy! Mrs. Judy!" the little ones called, their faces lighting up as they rushed to embrace her. She enveloped each child in a warm embrace of love, leaving an indelible mark on their hearts.

Mom breathed life into her children every single day, and her sister, Mrs. Joann, radiated beauty like a basket brimming with roses. "Her dazzling smile, like the sun's warm rays, lit up the entire property." I was a spirited and perceptive child with an unusual depth from the start. Everything intrigued me, and when Ryan arrived, I became a little scientist, examining him closely—from his oversized head to those tiny duck-like feet. Born in 1993, my little brother was utterly adorable. I cradled him on my lap, whispering comfort in the wake of schoolyard skirmishes, assuring him that all would be well. Brothers must be each other's protectors, especially when life throws its challenges.

As Proverbs 17:17 wisely says:

> A friend loves at all times, and a brother is born for adversity."

It's in those tough moments that a brother's true love shines through. If you have a brother, cherish him at every opportunity, not just during trials, for adversities will come—and when desperation knocks, who will be your beacon? I often reached out to friends in times of need, but it was my brother who always had my back. I'm not claiming that the bond of brotherhood can't exist among friends, but if it doesn't fit, don't force it. You shouldn't feel obligated to socialize with everyone for validation.

I write to express that God's love is eternal, unfaltering through every trial, obstacle, or mountain we face. Many of my friends battled various struggles—heart issues, seizures—and I wrestled with anxiety and depression, my own ongoing battle. Anxiety creeps in, born of being overwhelmed by the world's chaos and the worry of what tomorrow might bring. I recall as vividly as yesterday—Dad returning home every fortnight in his worn brown blazer, crisp white shirt, and tailored black pants, topped with a felt hat that screamed sophistication. Whenever I stepped out of line, that belt spoke louder than words. It wasn't the harshest of reprimands, but it left its mark. A simple "that's enough" from Mom would diffuse the situation, and he'd move on.

In my younger years, I wasn't a handful, but as I gained more freedom, life became a bit chaotic. I had a dear friend who lived in a cheerful yellow house with a white garage, his dad driving trucks while his mom had a magical touch, twisting my mother's hair into mesmerizing locks. We'd sneak into his room, eagerly watching music videos on BET, reveling in our innocence and longing for joy. His house rules were much looser than mine, explaining my frequent visits. In the early '90s, hip-hop culture was all about baggy pants, flashy chains, and golden smiles, but we had none of that. My circle of friends was raised in devotion, adhering to the teachings of God's kingdom, and so we understood that our parents would never allow us to indulge in just any entertainment.

Here I was, ensnared in a haze, feigning a version of myself that simply wasn't true, jeopardizing my liberty for a flurry of expletives and a dash of rhythmic movement. To my friends and family, let this serve as a reminder: never allow the pursuit of personal freedoms to lead you into the snares of sin. What then? Are we to sin just because we stand under grace and not the law? God forbid it. Do you not realize that whoever you choose to serve, that's who you truly belong to?

Whether you embrace the path of sin leading to death or choose obedience that drives you toward righteousness. Look closely—bit by bit, I found myself shackled by sin's grip because I craved the life I witnessed on glowing screens. Some parents shrugged off my obsessions with, "It's just a fad, it will fade," yet slowly, inevitably, I morphed into the image reflected back at me—a mere thug in the grand performance. This is not a critique of those who revel in hip hop or R&B, but heed this truth: don't wear a shoe if it doesn't fit!

How is it conceivable that God could mingle His angels with the devils of hell? It is not, for Satan himself, prideful and rebellious, stood against the Creator's design. Revelation tells us of the great dragon, that ancient serpent, known as the Devil, who deceives the entire world, cast down to earth along with his infernal followers. It isn't within God's desire that any should perish; rather, He yearns for us all to turn from our sins and seek Jesus.

Understand this, dear sons and daughters: you may

succeed in deceiving your parents, but divine eyes see you fully; there is no evading Him. The Lord is not slow to fulfill His promises, but is endlessly patient, not wishing for any soul to be lost, urging us toward repentance. The Lord had laden my life with promises, yet I stood unprepared to receive His abundant gifts. Beloved, I hope above all else that you thrive and find health, just as your soul flourishes. God's will is for His saints to prosper, but first, we must align ourselves—prepared to confront our challenges with resolve. Trials surfaced relentlessly.

Everything my mother warned of became my reality —I turned to theft, and in a dark twist, my own possessions were pilfered. I sought approval through conflict, yet God's voice echoed, "What you truly need is My acceptance." Too many of us scramble for validation in the fleeting and the tangible, reaching for material comforts devoid of meaning. Yet God beckons us to rest in His unfailing love during our hardest times. I recall the sting of taking what wasn't mine, only to find my own wallet missing days later, stripped of over three hundred dollars. My boss confronted me, saying, "I know it was you; return it, and I'll spare you legal trouble." Even then, God was watching over me, orchestrating my path toward redemption.

When I was about twenty, I found myself unwittingly swept into a chaotic gang brawl where over eleven guys pounced on me like feral beasts. The memory clings to my mind, as vivid as a scene from yesterday. It was a gloomy and isolating day; my friends and I sported twisted smirks, aware that trouble was brewing. We ventured into one of Louisiana's roughest neighborhoods, adrenaline surging through our veins. In a reckless moment, one of my pals swung a bat, shattering the teeth of a man lingering outside. It was a bold gamble, but ultimately foolish. Soon, the air thickened with tension as locals emerged to counter our provocation; after all, we had trespassed into their territory, and we were unmistakably looking for trouble.

I recall leaping from the car, weighing just a hundred and thirty pounds, knowing full well that I couldn't harm even the smallest insect, yet feeling audacious enough to dive headlong into the frenzy. A flurry of punches rained down on me, and I plummeted to the ground, experiencing the sickening impact of fists, boots, and makeshift weapons colliding with my face. Overwhelmed, I was trampled mercilessly, losing count after fifty violent stomps until darkness enveloped me. My cousin, the embodiment of loyalty, yanked me towards the car, bloodied and bewildered, adrift in confusion and barely clinging to life. I managed to croak out, "What happened?" as he sped towards the hospital, where I lay on the stark emergency room table.

The brain, I learned, is a delicate construct of blood vessels and nerves, cradled by cerebrospinal fluid meant to shield it from the infamous blow of the skull. But when that impact strikes, brain cells begin to perish in its wake, yielding a cascade of neurotransmitters erupting chaotically, leading to an agonizing overload—akin to a system crash inducing temporary paralysis. Yet, hear me when I say, despite being battered with a metal rod, and kicked senselessly, I stood here unbroken—no concussions, no lasting brain damage. A mere six months later, I emerged whole.

I am here to share that when a divine calling envelops your spirit, no weapon forged against you shall prevail.

(Isaiah 54:17) People conspired against me and whispered behind my back, yet when the Lord is at your side, who can stand against you? Prayer reigns as a formidable shield in the life of a believer, striking down the foes even before they dare to advance. Truly, it was the miracle-working power of God that pulled me back from the brink of death. The Scriptures affirm that the angel of the Lord stands guard, encamping around those who revere Him, delivering them from peril. (Psalm 34:7)

My mother's prayers were sent out to me that fateful day, and I am forever grateful to God for granting me survival. I want to remind you that your very survival is a testament to the divine purpose resting upon your life; He led you through the flames with intention and grace.

As it's written in Daniel 3:1, King Nebuchadnezzar forged a towering image of gold, measuring sixty cubits in height and six in breadth, erecting it in the plains of Dura, within Babylon's vast province. He then summoned the princes, governors, captains, judges, treasurers, counselors, sheriffs, and all the rulers of the provinces to come forth for the grand dedication of this golden idol he had set before the people. The great assembly gathered to pay homage, standing solemnly before the image Nebuchadnezzar so proudly claimed as his own.

Then a herald proclaimed loudly, "To you, O peoples, nations, and languages, it is hereby commanded that when you hear the sound of musical instruments—cornet, flute, harp, sackbut, psaltery, dulcimer, and every kind of music—you must fall down and worship the golden image the king has erected. And whosoever does not comply shall, at that very hour, be thrown into the heart of a blazing furnace." Among those defying the decree were three faithful Jews: Shadrach, Meshach, and Abednego. Introduced in verse twelve, they stood firm, disregarding the king's order. Enraged to discover their rebellion, King Nebuchadnezzar demanded they be cast into the fire. "What god can save you from my furnace?" he thundered.

But the three answered with valor, "O Nebuchadnezzar, we need not defend ourselves before you. Our God, whom we honor, is capable of rescuing us from the flames, and He will save us from your hands, O king." In his fury, the king ordered the furnace to be heated seven times hotter. The flames were so fierce that they consumed the soldiers who cast them in. Yet, when Nebuchadnezzar peered into the inferno, he beheld four figures walking unscathed, one resembling the Son of God. Astonished, he leaped up and called to his advisers, "Did we not cast in three men bound into the flames?" They affirmed it was so. "Look! I see four men walking freely in the fire, unharmed, and the fourth is like a divine being."

I want to remind you that God is meticulous about accompanying you through the flames of adversity. The Bible vividly declares that amidst the roaring fire, not even a single hair on their heads was singed, nor did their garments carry the slightest trace of smoke; they emerged unscathed and untouched! Isn't it utterly miraculous to recognize that in your most fiery trials, God walks beside you? He would never abandon you to the merciless heat, but instead allows the enemy to crank up the temperature sevenfold, revealing His unparalleled might! Instead of pleading with God to whisk you away from the blazes, implore Him to intensify the heat—so you may witness the fullness of

His divine power on display! Consider the fate of the faithful: not only did they endure the inferno, but the very king decreed that any soul who dared to speak ill of the God of Shadrach, Meshach, and Abednego would face dire consequences.

> So, I declare this decree: That every people, nation, and language which dares utter a word against the God of Shadrach, Meshach, and Abednego shall be cut into pieces, and their homes turned to rubble, for there is no other God capable of such deliverance.
>
> DANIEL 3:29

Reflect on my own journey; when I was saved, God transformed even those who had cursed Him and trampled upon my existence into instruments of His glory. They would gaze in astonishment, wondering, "How is it that he yet lives?" They thought they had me conquered, but God assured me, "I have forged an unbreakable covenant with him from before the foundations of the world." What does it truly mean to enter into a covenant? A covenant, dear friends, is defined as a solemn, sacred union between God and man. It transcends the mere nature of a contract; contracts are temporary and can crumble under pressure. A covenant is designed to endure eternally. When God established a covenant with Abraham, He promised that through him, all his descendants would be blessed. "I will bless those who bless you, and whoever curses you I will curse, and all people on earth will be blessed through you." You see, a covenant is not easily cast aside, because God is not like a man who falters in promise.

When God pledges something to you, you can anchor your hope in that assurance. I recall when my mother received the revelation that I would one day find salvation. Each night, when I stumbled home in a drunken haze, she gently laid me to rest, speaking words of life over me. She clung to the promise that the same God who initiated a good work in me would undoubtedly bring it to completion. Philippians 1:6 assures us:

> "Being confident of this, that he who began a good work in you will carry it on to completion until the day of Christ Jesus."

God yearns to bring you to fulfillment, but first, you must step aside. An unwilling vessel will thwart His efforts. Many years slipped by where I was ensnared in complacency, stationary and unyielding, my heart unwilling to reach for more, while God demanded greater depths from me. At twenty-one, I entered into matrimony with my childhood sweetheart, yet our union crumbled in a mere month. We engaged in torrents of arguments, and soon, she chose to leave. Where division takes root, a home cannot withstand the tumult, for without the foundation of Christ, it is bound to fail.

> "And if a house is divided against itself, that house will not be able to stand."
>
> MARK 3:25

Where there are two conflicting visions within a household, division is bound to emerge. It's like an unseen enemy creeping in, sowing seeds of strife that quickly flourish, overshadowing the love of God that should unify. The solemn vows we exchanged, our "I do's," held a depth we had scarcely understood, for we were blissfully unaware of the trials that lay ahead. The moment we bound ourselves together before God, the enemy smirked mockingly, challenging the Creator: "They won't be able to stand united for Your glory."

Whenever God aims to extract glory from our lives, the adversary, in his relentless pursuit, launches an all-out attack, desperately trying to infiltrate our homes. To dismantle a covenant is to dismantle a legacy. Take Eve, for instance; the enemy targeted her in the garden, fully aware of her vulnerabilities. If he could maneuver her into betraying God, he could ensnare Adam as well. My ex-wife and I mirrored Adam and Eve in ways we couldn't have imagined. We took a bite from the forbidden fruit—an act defying God's clear mandate. Instead of having honest conversations to uncover the roots of our discord, we devolved into chaos, like wild beasts fighting with one another, consumed by our pain and bitterness. My ex-wife turned to another, seeking solace in another man's arms, building a life with him while our covenant lay in tatters. If anyone had a reason to throw in the towel, it should have been me. Yet, stewing in the depths of despair, I chose a different path. Instead of surrendering to vices like alcohol or drugs to numb my suffering, I sought God in prayer and fasting. Miraculously, He granted me the fortitude to endure.

The birth of my daughter on September 2, 2011, illuminated my life with unmatched brilliance—a beacon of hope amidst darkness. Yet I ventured back to the heart of the matter and observed how my daughter's formative years became entwined with influences that distorted her understanding of a father. From house to house, stepfather to stepfather, the stability I longed to provide seemed perpetually out of reach. Her mother caught up in a haze of smoking and drinking, left me plagued with worries about our daughter's safety and well-being. I watched helplessly as my little girl departed with others who could not fathom the sanctity of shared responsibility.

During this tumultuous period, God whispered to me, urging me to remain still, trusting that He would be my strength. I determined not to fight back against her, even as her anger transformed into speartips hurled at my character, igniting gossip and scheming from the community around us. They conspired against me, even orchestrating a setup involving a soldier, yet miraculously, none of the accusations found their mark. None of their weapons prospered because, in that moment of despair, the Spirit of God rose like a standard against the flood of negativity. Isaiah 59:19—"So shall they fear the name of the Lord from the west, and His glory from the rising of the sun. When the enemy shall come in like a flood, the Spirit of the Lord shall lift up a standard against him"—became a lifeline for me. Through the storm my ex-wife conjured, my self-esteem took a beating, shattering to the point where I felt unworthy even to step outside. Her friends and family, with their skewed perceptions of who I was, further distorted my image in the eyes of the world. When gossip festers and spreads, it can obliterate lives, leaving haunting shadows in its wake. The pain of distortion settled in my heart, yet I held onto the hope that truth would prevail.

I remained silent in the face of my enemies. Instead, I chose to slay them with kindness, harnessing the profound wisdom found in scripture. As it is written in Luke 6:28, "Bless those who curse you, and pray for those who mistreat you." This command invites a radical transformation of the heart. When we pray for our adversaries, we invite divine intervention, allowing God to soften their hearts towards us. It becomes a divine exchange—our closeness to God strengthens us, rendering the injuries that once ravaged our spirits powerless. I could stand before those who called themselves my friends, all the while fully aware of their betrayal, the infidelity that pierced my heart. Yet, I would look them in the eye and utter, "God bless you." This act of grace underscores our true measure of strength and our connection to the divine—reflected in the way we treat those who oppose us.

Consider the journey of David. King Saul, consumed by jealousy, hurled spears in malice towards him, yet scriptural truth reveals a deeper narrative. An evil spirit plagued Saul, and what did David do? He did not retaliate; he fought his battles with the weapon of praise. God utilizes our gifts to not only heal us but can transform our foes through our very testimonies. 1 Samuel 16:23 states, "And it came to pass, when the evil spirit from God was upon Saul, that David took a harp, and played with his hand: so Saul was refreshed and was well, and the evil spirit departed from him."

How magnificent it is that music—a gift from God—calmed the storm within. The maidens sang, "Saul has slain his thousands, and David his ten thousands," sparking jealousy in Saul's heart. We must guard ourselves against the insidious spirit of envy, for it may blind us to the blessings that God aims to bestow upon us through those whom we would otherwise wish ill. Rather than returning strikes, David chose to comfort and soothe Saul with his melody. Throughout my tumultuous life—a life shaped by divorce, the shadow of armed robberies, altercations, and looming threats against my existence—I recognize that it has been God lifting me above these tribulations. "If God be for us, who can be against us?" became my mantra. Since accepting Him into my life, I have cast aside my stubbornness, allowing faith to mold my perspective.

CHAPTER TWO

FROM CONVENIENT TO COVENANT

The term "convenient" refers to that which perfectly fits our personal desires, needs, and routines—a mere selection of choices available to us. But God calls us to something greater, a divine ordination.

Following my salvation in 2011, I shifted from merely pursuing what was convenient for me to seeking His ordained purpose with fervor. When we cling solely to convenience, we risk capping the limitless scope of God's blessings, diving only into His shallow waters instead of the ocean He intends for us. Consider the ache of guilt that often accompanies premarital intimacy, a disconnect from God's intentions, leaving many feeling unworthy and unfulfilled.

Loneliness is a universal plight, a shadow that visits us all. Yet, when we trade the covenantal bonds God designed for fleeting substitutes, we tarnish the image God intended to portray through families. Marriage exists as a canvas to showcase His glory, reflecting His purpose and covenant love amidst our earthly existence. Why, then, do we sacrifice His ordination for mere temporal pleasures? It is because, within the body of Christ, we seem to have lost the ability to wait upon the Lord, yearning for instant gratification rather than the divine fulfillment He promises in His perfect timing.

> "But they that wait upon the Lord shall renew their strength; they shall mount up with wings as eagles; they shall run, and not be weary; and they shall walk, and not faint."
>
> ISAIAH 40:31

In moments of quiet contemplation, when we place our trust in God, we are gifted with a strength that transcends our understanding. The Almighty does not desire us to rush into a relationship with Him half-formed or underdeveloped but instead wishes for us to grow deliberately and faithfully.

> "And this I pray, that your love may abound yet more and more in knowledge and in all judgment; That ye may approve things that are excellent; that ye may be sincere and without offense till the day of Christ."
>
> PHILIPPIANS 1:9-10

God longs for our love to flourish, to become a vibrant force that empowers us to discern wisely in our choices. He beckons us to embrace sincerity, a commitment to uphold divine principles in our everyday lives. As I journeyed deeper in my faith, I found myself shedding the old self, akin to shedding a worn-out garment, and embracing the new man described in Ephesians 4:22-24:

> That ye put off concerning the former conversation the old man, which is corrupt according to the deceitful lusts; And be renewed in the spirit of your mind; And that ye put on the new man, which after God is created in righteousness and true holiness."

The Scriptures assert that the old self is tainted and dwindling, and I knew I could not return to those outdated patterns of living. The temptations of intimacy outside God's design, the allure of excess—these were not worth sacrificing my communion with the Creator for fleeting moments of pleasure.

The reality is that indulging in fleeting desires like casual relationships can lead to a life filled with pitfalls and unanswered regrets. It can erode a man's true essence and impede his ability to walk in the strength of his divine masculinity. Mankind was crafted with purpose, designed to thrive under the governance of God. Straying from this divine alignment diminishes a man's innate potential. Sure, we often conjure excuses, rationalizing why we fall short daily, but continuous sin is not meant to be our norm.

Romans 6:1-2 chimes in:

> What shall we say then? Shall we continue in sin, that grace may abound? God forbid. How shall we, that are dead to sin, live any longer therein?"

If we are truly dead to past cravings, how can we repeatedly stumble along that familiar, destructive path? My resolve as a servant of God is to set a standard for what it means to live righteously. I do not hunger for convenience; I aspire for covenant! The allure of what is easy can corrode marriages, suffocate our hopes, and leave us in despair. It can tear apart our very being, leading us through a maze of deceit and heartache. I have stumbled countless times, but through these trials, I have learned the importance of remaining sheltered within God's embrace, attuning my heart to His guiding presence.

God is vibrantly alive, a living, breathing essence that spans the heavens and envelops the Earth in infinite embrace. He observes every heartbeat, every whisper of the world, ensuring that not a single soul goes unnoticed. His omnipresence means He exists in every nook and cranny of existence; yes, even in your home, lovingly watching over your family and those you cherish deeply. In the sacred verses of Psalm 91, when David exhorts us to dwell in the secret sanctuary of the Most High, he speaks to the profound power of prayer.

> "To rest in that secret place is to abide under the protective shadow of the Almighty, a refuge that nourishes the soul.
>
> PSALM 91:1

It is crucial for you to align your spirit to the divine, for many of us, in our restless wanderings, are tossed like leaves by every passing breeze of doctrine, allowing the chaos of the world to cloud our minds. Consider the term "television program"; it's not a mere coincidence. These "programs" are crafted to shape your thoughts to influence your understanding of reality. This is why it is essential to flood your mind with the strength and wisdom found in the Word of God, cleansing it of the noise so that you might reflect His image in a world so eager for conformity.

Distractions are plentiful in modern society; God's sanctity and His Word hold tremendous value that must never be compromised. When we choose to forsake God's best, embracing things that glitter but are not satisfying, we risk diminishing our discernment and missing the wonderful ways in which God is at work in our lives. He is a Spirit of vastness and omnipresence, and he carries the responsibility of watching over all of humanity, including all His beloved children. Psalm 24 resonates with truth:

> The earth is the Lord's, and the fullness thereof; the world, and they that dwell therein."

He has established the realm, creating it with purpose. In order for us to walk in victory through this life, a yielded relationship with God is essential. However, many have molded themselves to the world, adopting its measures and standards; they wear the world's scent and yet lament their lack of blessings. This occurs because they have loosened their grip on God's divine standard of holiness—a standard that is pure and untainted. Holiness is defined by His perfect nature. When God looks at you, He sees you through the lens of His love, recognizing you as His own precious creation.

Do not allow anything to come between you and His love. Romans 12:2 implores us:

> "And be not conformed to this world: but be ye transformed by the renewing of your mind, that ye may prove what is that good, and acceptable, and perfect will of God."

To conform is to yield, to fall subject to external forces that dictate your path. You stand either in the dominion of your inherent sinful nature or under the influence of God's Holy Spirit. As you resist the pull of the flesh, you begin to immerse yourself in the rich soil of God's kingdom. You start to embrace His divine words, becoming intricately linked to His nature. Peter beautifully illustrates this connection in his letters to the early church; he reminds us of our grafting into God's kingdom. Know this: God longs for you to grasp the precious promises He extends, promises that can only thrive through His Word.

2 Peter 1:3-4 assures us of His provision:

> "3 As His divine power grants us everything that pertains to life and godliness through the knowledge of Him who calls us to glories and virtues; 4 We have been given magnificent and precious promises, so that through them, we might partake of His divine nature, escaping the corruption in the world fueled by desires."

The term "divine" embodies a sense of excellence and delight. When you ascend to the pinnacle of excellence in

God, you find yourself enveloped in the gentle embrace of humility. This marks your initial steps toward embodying the essence of "as He is." There exists a realm within this world where the chains of fleshly corruption can be cast off entirely, allowing you to attain an incorruptible state, forever in communion with your Heavenly Father.

A divine nature emanating from God acts as a liberating force from the sin that seeks to ensnare. This transformation first ignited within my mind. As I delved deeper into God's word, I began to shed the old mindsets that clung to me like shadows, for each day became a little easier, a little clearer, as the voice of God resonated with increasing clarity within me. I found a job at Ul Parking and Transit, and as my relationship with God blossomed, so too did the anointing I carried; I transformed into a formidable presence within God's kingdom. His promises, once distant echoes, began to materialize before my eyes.

Each day, I heard His voice through His scriptures, guiding me with a spirit of discernment as I learned to navigate the shifting dynamics around me, identifying those in need of prayer. I became an active seeker of souls, and one fateful day, I encountered a girl who seemed lost amidst the throngs of people—a beautiful spirit yearning for connection, whom we'll refer to as Jodi. Jodi was hesitant about men, a result of past wounds that left her heart bruised, yet beneath her guarded exterior lay a profound longing for a savior. The human spirit innately craves reunion with its Creator.

I began to speak life and scripture into her existence, watching as the chains of her bondages disintegrated, and slowly, like a flower reaching towards the sun, her smile began to emerge, brightening her countenance. Our friendship flourished because we chose to live not by the dictates of the flesh. We intentionally distanced ourselves from temptation, gathering for fervent prayer meetings that ushered in mighty deliverances for both of us, setting us free from the strongholds that had once shackled us. I never sought credit for those I ministered to—I recognized that I was but a sower of seeds.

The Bible reassures us that when we sow, it is God who provides the increase, the transformation of mere seeds into vibrant life. As articulated in 1 Corinthians 3:6-8, "I have planted, Apollos watered; but God gave the increase." Our efforts, while necessary, are insignificant without the divine touch, for it is God who orchestrates the growth and vitality of what is planted.

Living as a man wholly committed to Christ is a daunting challenge. It compels you to relinquish your own belief systems and don the mindset of Christ Himself. This metamorphosis occurs through immersion in His word—His teachings serve as a protective covering that fosters a new outlook on life. I began to expect miracles, believing wholeheartedly that when burdens of illness, such as cancer, arose, my prayers could facilitate healing. This faith fueled a connection that proved powerful, and through prayer, people found healing and restoration in the arms of God's grace.

There were countless moments of solitude where words failed to capture the depths of my emotions, and in those times, I turned to God. The heartache of a painful separation in 2012 ultimately culminated in a divorce in 2014. Still, through it all, the steadfast love and guidance of God proved to be my solace and strength, knitting together the fabric of my spirit into something even more resilient, reflective of His unwavering light.

I found myself on an excruciating emotional rollercoaster during that tumultuous period of my life, experiencing dizzying heights of joy and crushing depths of despair. It was as if each moment was marked by stabs to my very soul. I would often ponder, "How can I face the future of watching my daughter blossom into the incredible person she is meant to be without her father by her side?" Moments of hopelessness crept in like shadows. Yet, amidst the chaos, God's voice resonated within me, directing me to extend blessings even to those who sought my demise.

With soft-spoken responses that danced in the air like whispered prayers, I encountered the disdain of those who thrived on negativity aimed at me. One by one, I witnessed divine justice unfold, humbling them in ways only God can orchestrate. Such is the nature of a just God; He turns the tide, making those who once pressed against you become unlikely allies.

Today, I wish to remind you, dear reader, that there are still mountains to climb and victories to be achieved in your life. Despite the challenges that rattled my core, I committed myself to my work, diligently pouring my energy into my labor. My income flourished, and through the trials of my divorce, I unearthed what it truly meant to be a man of integrity and strength.

The scriptures wisely caution us against viewing these daunting tests as unusual, for they are, in fact, an intrinsic part of our spiritual journey. So, I urge you—to grasp the steadfast hand of God and refuse to let go. As 1 Peter 4:12-13 assures us:

> "Beloved, think it not strange concerning the fiery trial which is to try you, as though some strange thing happened unto you: But rejoice, inasmuch as ye are partakers of Christ's sufferings; that when his glory shall be revealed, ye may be glad also with exceeding joy."

Each day offers a new opportunity for rejoicing in our transformed nature; it manifests as we discover patience, attend to our responsibilities at home, and eagerly open our hearts to receive the Word of the Lord.

When my wife unexpectedly departed, instead of succumbing to the weight of stress, I turned to God with an insatiable yearning. My prayers became symphonies as if angels trumpeted melodies in the heavenly realms, and I was blessed with sacred visitations during my meditations with the Lord. In one extraordinary instance, I found myself enveloped in a swirling confusion—a darkness pressing in from all sides—until suddenly, a brilliant light pierced through, illuminating my path with heavenly clarity. Through this radiant portal, I stepped into an expansive forest teeming with the malevolent spirits of adversity. Armed with the sword of truth, I charged forward; each swing of my blade vanquished foes who dared to challenge me. The deeper I ventured into the woods, the more formidable my adversaries became—but simultaneously, my sword grew stronger. This sword is a metaphor for the Word of God, ever potent in our lives.

You may face countless opponents, yet armed with Scripture, you can battle against legions of despair and defeat. Let us now discuss the profound nature of the divine covenant. When God establishes a covenant with you, He lays the foundation of a promise that can never be broken. He declares, "Son, I will grant you a fulfilled life, overflowing with blessings, if you align yourself with my will." As 1 Peter 2:2 beautifully encourages, "As newborn babes, desire the sincere milk of the word, that ye may grow thereby." Progress may begin slowly, but commit to reading a chapter daily. In time, the scriptures will weave themselves into the very fabric of your heart.

The Word acts as a discerning sword, cutting through the layers of the heart and initiating a profound inward transformation. By the conclusion of my vision, I found myself among the strongest in the land, impervious to any demonic force. This same miraculous power, this fortitude in faith, awaits every Christian willing to seize it today.his word is the power that can reshape reality, breathing life and potential into the most barren of souls. You engage in a profound mental exercise, etching His word deep within your spirit, allowing it to resonate through every thought and breath.

The act of vocalizing this divine truth is where miracles begin, for the scriptures reveal the extraordinary strength held within our speech. Take heed of Proverbs 18:21 in the King James Version, which boldly proclaims,

> Death and life are in the power of the tongue: and they that love it shall eat the fruit thereof."

In those moments when people encounter me, wide-eyed and curious, they often exclaim, "Aren't you just the most positive person?" or "Where does your fierce spirit come from?" I smile and simply respond, “It’s all about God.”

This covenant with the Most High breeds an awe-inspiring reverence for the gift of life. Whether you have tasted the bitter dregs of addiction, been left for dead by circumstance, or faced the heartbreak of abandonment in childhood, know this: God's love surpasses all understanding, enveloping you in a warmth beyond your wildest dreams. Transitioning from pursuing what is merely convenient to embracing what is sacred in covenant opens the floodgates to the endless promises of God, saturating your being with blessings that once seemed unreachable.

With God, those dreams that felt like distant shores transform into solid ground beneath your feet, easily within your grasp. He desires that you experience richness in both mind and spirit, showering you with the bountiful joys that come from his divine law. When we enter into this sacred covenant, it’s as if a treasure chest of God's blessings unlocks before us, inviting us to revel in the life He has tirelessly fought for us to possess. We start to embody the essence of true men and women of God, standing resolute against the standards of worldly living that seek to define us. A covenant is not just a fleeting promise; it is a lifelong commitment.

When God establishes a covenant, be prepared for an outpouring of miracles, signs, and wonders to dance through the pathway of your life. Covenant brings forth an enduring relationship with God that stands the test of time. Consider Job, who made a solemn covenant with his eyes to avoid even the thought of lust and, in doing so, earned the boundless blessings of God. As Job articulated in Job 31:1, "I made a covenant with mine eyes; why then should I think upon a maid?" His covenant stemmed from a life lived blamelessly before God, and I remind you today that the same God who honored Job is the God who walks with you.

In the realm of covenant, God looks beyond our flaws and shortcomings rather than beholding His promises fulfilled in our lives. I, too, have made a covenant, this one with my daughter, declaring that I would never forsake her, a commitment woven with love and unwavering support. A fulfilled covenant brings not only satisfaction but liberation, lifting you from the chains of complacency and propelling you into the magnificent experiences God has prepared for you. He is taking you on a journey from faith to faith and glory to glory, as beautifully captured in 2 Corinthians 3:18:

> “But we all, with open face beholding as in a glass the glory of the Lord, are changed into the same image from glory to glory, even as by the Spirit of the Lord.”

It is the Spirit of the Most High that metamorphoses a man from an alcoholic into a fervent believer, a courageous warrior for God, equipped to chase down demons that stalk the shadows. The transformative Spirit of God takes a battered, bruised woman. It refines her into the radiant person He has always envisioned her to be, awakening the divine purpose planted in her heart. I write this with a heart full of gratitude for you. You, who have chosen to forsake the fleeting comforts of convenience for the steadfast embrace of the covenant, will find that the riches of heaven await you.

This journey we call covenant is not one defined by

fear or drenched in doubt, for indeed, it is written that God's perfect love drives out all fear, replacing it with a profound peace. Let me take you back to a time that loomed dark in my memory, a place where shadows danced around me and the weight of despair felt all-consuming. It is here that I truly felt the transformative love of God lifting me from the abyss. There were moments, several in fact when His love for me was so immense that it rescued me from certain peril.

One night stands out, shrouded in coldness and darkness, the kind where the moon hides behind thick clouds, shivering under the weight of night—a night that still stirs the depths of my soul. I had just ventured out from my hotel room, drawn by a simple craving for refreshment. Setting foot on the pavement, I was met with an eerie stillness as I walked briskly toward the gas station, each step echoing in the silence of the hour. Suddenly, from the shadows emerged a figure draped in a long white t-shirt and dark pants, his demeanor unsettling. "Do you have any marijuana on you?" he asked, his voice low and laced with menace.

"No, I don't," I replied, my heart pounding, innocent yet oblivious, lost in the throes of my own ignorance about the hour—two o'clock in the morning, and I was utterly alone. His gaze bore into me, a chilling blank stare that froze me in place. Then, in a harrowing heartbeat, a second figure sprinted from behind him, brandishing a black pistol, a demand spilling from his lips for my money. "I don't have any money," I stammered, panic thrumming in my veins. The first man—now circling me like a predator—lashed out, his fist connecting with my face again and again. "Give up the money!" he barked.

My world spun as if I had stepped onto a carousel of despair, dizzy and disoriented. "Get out of the car," the gunman commanded, and in that instant, I could only hope, fervently, that somehow, I would survive this ordeal. With my heart pounding, I willed myself to move, peeling myself from the safety of my car, face pale and trembling. I caught a flicker of relief watching the man turn his gaze away, if only for a split second. That was my moment. I bolted, adrenaline surging through me, dashed across a ditch, my clothes soaking in cold water. I barely noticed in my flight that I had kicked off a shoe in my frantic escape.

Glancing back, I saw the man who had no gun chasing me, but out of nowhere came the voice piercing through the chaos, "Let him go." I could hardly grasp the weight of those words as gratitude flooded my heart. Once more, I thanked the Lord. His angels had encamped around me, shielding me from harm when I needed it most, just as they had done countless times before. Like Job, I sensed the divine decree: "You can take his belongings, but his life remains untouched." Emerging from that harrowing night, I found gratitude blossoming inside me.

Trouble has a way of lifting the veil from our eyes and teaching us to appreciate the simplest blessings—the gentle rustle of leaves, the warmth of a smile, the sweetness of laughter. The material comforts of America often leave us yearning for more; we become spoiled by abundance and lose sight of the true richness found in faith and gratitude. Even as I traversed the path toward spiritual maturity, the vital importance of community shone through. I leaned into the embrace of my church brothers, their unwavering love and support acting as a lifeline. They wanted the best for me, and I reveled in their wisdom.

In moments of trial, we often overlook one pivotal lesson—patience. The rush for immediate satisfaction clouds our understanding of value, and we forget that true blessings come with time, cultivated through endurance and faithfulness. It's a dance of waiting and trusting, a rhythm in God's timing that leads us to the treasures we seek. If one is fortunate enough to receive something freely given, it might lead to a heartless full of gratitude compared to when one has toiled and labored, pouring sweat and soul into the endeavor.

As reflected in the wisdom of 2 Peter 3:9, which reminds us that the Lord does not slacken in His promises, we must understand that His long-suffering is borne out of love, wishing for no soul to drift away but instead inviting all into the grace of repentance. Patience, dear reader, is not merely an exercise but an invitation. From a place of unease and impatience, we can transform into vessels of hope, receiving the bountiful promises God lays before us. We are called to steadfastness, to wait on Him with courage unfurling in our hearts, for He assures us that our wait is not in vain.

His strength shines most vividly in our moments of frailty; I saw this truth unfold vividly in my journey. After the traumatic incident of the robbery, when I felt the weight of fear and vulnerability press down upon me, I did not succumb. Instead, I reached for that flicker of faith and called the authorities. The line-up—a parade of five—yielded the faces of two men who threatened my peace. This moment, rather than breaking me, rebirthed an undying gratitude within as I recognized God's hand guarding me with His grace and mercy, like a shield amidst the chaos.

This newfound assurance led me to distinguish between desires that merely sounded enticing and blessings that truly nourished my spirit. I learned that not every acquaintance was trustworthy and that it was wise for me to retreat from the night's darkness. Each lesson was an impartation of divine wisdom, and it coalesced into a profound realization: I was called to a higher path. Soon, with a spirit overflowing with faith, I surrendered my life to Jesus Christ and embarked on a journey unlike any other I had known!

By the time my divorce came crashing into my world, I was no longer the person I once was. I had grown in maturity, leaning into God's will and recognizing that authentic promotion emanated not from an earthly title or job but directly from His sovereign hand. As articulated in Psalm 75:6-7, the rise and fall of man ultimately lie in the judgment of God, who promotes one and humbles another. Embracing that truth, I witnessed God propel me forward in my career, distinguishing me as a leader within my community.

This newfound leadership wasn't just a title; it was a call to be an activist for Christian rights, a torchbearer for faith, ensuring God's glory radiated through every action I took. I returned to college, fueled not just by ambition but by a fervent desire to reflect the transformative power of the Almighty. Like Paul, I grasped the necessity of releasing the past to seize what God had prepared ahead of me. In Philippians 3:13, it's laid bare: we are not to linger in yesterday's shadows but to stretch forth toward the dawn of fresh opportunities laid before us.

We are urged to persevere despite the burdens we

carry. I stood in the rubble of my brokenness, yet even there, I sensed God using that very fragility to crystallize His glory in my life. The book of James enlightens us about patience—that it's not an empty wait but a crafting process for our characters. In James 1:2-3, we're encouraged to embrace joy amid diverse trials, knowing that our faith's trials cultivate patience.

So many struggle, defeated, with the narrative they weave—that God has forsaken them. Yet what I discovered is that our perceptions can mislead us. When James exhorts us to count it all joy, he beckons us to adopt an attitude of gratitude, revealing that every trial is a testament of God, deeming us worthy of growth and refinement. We should cherish those moments, recognizing them as divine appointments meant to fortify our spirits. Rejoice when the world seems to turn away from you, for in those moments, God surrounds you with steadfast friends who offer love without conditions, illuminating your path as you journey onward in faith.

Rejoice in the moments when life takes a turn, such as losing a job, for it is in these trials that God unveils a broader and more extraordinary plan for you. Find joy in the moments when others misinterpret or mistreat you; it is through these experiences that God is extracting every ounce of purpose from your life. Consider the transformation of grapes, squeezed to create fine wine, and olives, which are pressed, shaken, and beaten to yield the precious oil. This divine process of shaping and molding is God's way of preparing you for blessings untold! Seek completeness in God rather than in the material abundance that this world offers. Remember Matthew 24:35, where it is declared, "Heaven and earth shall pass away, but my words shall not pass away." Everything we encounter in this earthly existence is fleeting and temporary.

Jobs can come and go, but true happiness is an everlasting treasure. God desires His children to bask in joy, fulfilling their spirits through Him, as He desires to see us prosper in every aspect of our lives. Everything rests in the hands of our Creator, as emphasized in Psalm 24:1, which states, "The earth is the Lord's, and the fulness thereof; the world, and they that dwell therein." He laid the foundations of the earth and possesses intimate knowledge of all that inhabits it. Just as He granted Adam the gift of naming the creatures of the earth—finding fulfillment in that divine responsibility—so too must we discover satisfaction in the pursuits God has set before us.

The world may promise fulfillment but often delivers only stress and turmoil, which is far from what God desires for His beloved children. Fulfillment is about reaching completion; to experience it, we must cultivate a vibrant prayer life. Prayer is our lifeline in our journey with God, as stated in Luke 18:1, that "men ought always to pray, and not to faint." Through prayer, we are fortified against despair, ensuring we do not falter in difficult times. Trials are an inescapable part of life, yet with a dedicated prayer practice, the burdens we carry become lighter and our hearts more buoyant. God invites us to cast all our concerns upon Him, for He is prepared to handle them with love and care.

The pathway to joy is paved with prayer—God intimately knows our every need. He stands as a companion to the lonely, a nurturing father to the needy son, and a comforting mother to the broken-hearted daughter. In God, we find the fullness of everything we seek. To truly flourish, we must prioritize our relationship with our Heavenly Father above all else. As I nurtured this connection, I grew in strength and spirit, feeling the divine presence surrounding me more intensely than ever before. Each step I took outside my door was accompanied by His unwavering companionship, a constant reminder that I am never alone. God is with me, guiding my journey and enveloping me in His love. In this sacred relationship, I found the ultimate fulfillment, an unshakeable joy that transcends every circumstance that life may throw my way.

There comes a pivotal moment in every Christian's journey—a moment when familiar faces, those you believed would stand beside you through thick and thin, begin to fade away. Yet, take heart, for this shift is orchestrated for your greater good. You see, not everyone shares your yearning for a close relationship with God. As you draw nearer to Him, some may be swept away by the deceptive whispers of the enemy, revealing the truth that they might not have been genuine friends after all. So, do not burden your heart with worry or despair. When your fulfillment is anchored in God, you tap into a reservoir of blessings that overflow into every facet of your life.

The enemy, desperate to rob you of your joy, will launch a barrage of insidious thoughts filled with doubt and fear. If you allow him even a moment to influence your mind, he can turn your perception of life upside down. Instead of succumbing to these lies, rise and cast down those thoughts, dragging them into the light of God's truth. Reflect on the words of 2 Corinthians 10:5, which remind us of the power we possess through Christ to reclaim our minds and direct our thoughts towards obedience and righteousness.

Anything that attempts to elevate itself above the majesty of God must be cast down. When feelings of inadequacy creep in, refuse to let them take root—replace those shadows with the brilliant light of God's word.

Remember that God alone is true, sovereign, and eternal. He watches over you with unwavering diligence, both day and night, forever alert and attentive to His children's needs. "Hast thou not known? Hast thou not heard," the Scriptures remind us, "that the everlasting God, the LORD, the Creator of the ends of the earth, fainteth not, neither is weary?" (Isaiah 40:28). His wisdom is unfathomable, and His strength never ceases. Embrace each day like an exquisite gift, living as if it were your last, conforming your life to God's word, and inviting His transformative power to shape who you are.

God's divine power is formidable, capable of shaking the very foundations of your existence, transforming heartache and confusion into profound joy and serene peace. In the sacred space of His presence, search for the joy that rekindles your spirit. Understand that while you may feel a void, it is God Himself who longs to fill that emptiness—He is the ultimate fulfillment of every yearning heart. He embodies everlasting joy and is simply all that is good.

You are faced with a choice: will you pursue the world's fleeting ways, or will you seek the life that flows from God? You can find sustenance in the meager offerings of the world, or you can feast on the abundant blessings provided by your Creator. God's provision far surpasses anything the world can offer; His abundance is limitless, a vast ocean of grace that is beyond comprehension. If you tether yourself daily to your Heavenly Father, victory is your inheritance. But remember, victory comes with a price.

So the fundamental question beckons: will you humble yourself under the mighty hand of God, or will you strive to reign supreme over your own world? I speak from personal experience; were I to attempt reigning over my own life, I would have stumbled and fallen long ago. As it is written in Jeremiah 10:23, "O LORD, I know that the way of man is not in himself: it is not in man that walketh to direct his steps." Embrace this truth, my friend, for it is through surrender that we discover true strength and guidance in the divine embrace of our Creator.

When you attempt to steer your own course through life, you inadvertently restrain the hand of God that wishes to guide you. During a profound moment in a Bible study, I expressed a truth that resonates deeply: "It's not that God lacks power; rather, we fail to trust Him at His word." The Almighty is ever patient, waiting for you to grasp His promise so He may unveil His remarkable strength and unfathomable Glory in your existence. The magnificent Glory of God has the potential to be realized in your life through fasting and sincere prayer as God ardently yearns to showcase His splendor.

Now, let us consider the very essence of Glory—it embodies magnificence and great beauty. God's magnificence is unparalleled; it is the kind of magnificence that can transform the life of a drug addict, leading them toward a life of sobriety. His Glory is brilliantly displayed in the lives of those who are touched by Him. The Scriptures assert that salvation has the power to render a person beautiful; it adorns you with the grace of salvation itself. Psalm 149:4 beautifully articulates this, stating, "For the LORD takes pleasure in His people; He will beautify the meek with salvation." Ladies, walk through life with your heads held high, knowing you are radiant in the eyes of God. Your salvation is your finest adornment. And men, wear your humility as a cloak, understanding that God's glory molds you into the men you have become.

In this divine journey, we encounter varying levels of faith and expressions of Glory. The pivotal question remains, "How deeply do you trust Him?" Are you willing to trust Him enough to embark on a journey of sacrifice, echoing Abraham's unwavering faith in God, even at the expense of your children's well-being?

Let's delve into that remarkable passage from the scriptures: Genesis 22 opens with a profound moment when God tested Abraham. He called out, "Abraham!" to which Abraham warmly replied, "Here I am." Then, God issued a chilling command: "Take your son, your only son, whom you love—Isaac—and go to the region of Moriah. Sacrifice him there as a burnt offering on a mountain I will show you." Abraham gazed toward the distant place and instructed his servants to remain behind. A crucial lesson emerged: not everyone is destined to accompany you on the path God has laid out for you. Yes, it is human to desire the presence of friends and family as we navigate our journeys, yet we must remember—many are called, but few are chosen. This sentiment echoes in Matthew 22:14, reminding us of the sacred nature of divine selection.

Abraham gathered all he needed for this daunting sacrifice. As he approached the mountain, he laid the wood upon Isaac's back, leaving the boy perplexed, no doubt filled with questions of what was transpiring. Abraham took the wood for the burnt offering and placed it on Isaac while he himself carried the fire and the knife. And as they walked together, Isaac curiously asked, "Father?" to which Abraham promptly responded, "Yes, my son?" "The fire and wood are here," Isaac noted, "but where is the lamb for the burnt offering?" In that moment of profound faith, Abraham replied, "God Himself will provide the lamb for the burnt offering, my son." And so they continued their ascent up the mountain, guided by faith.

As they climbed, the narrative takes a poignant turn in Genesis 22:9—Abraham laid the wood over his son, demonstrating his incredible obedience to God. The Scriptures then reveal a pivotal moment when God called out to Abraham, commanding him to halt: "Stop!" This was a divine test of obedience, a moment crafted by God to assess whether Abraham would place his faith in Him wholeheartedly. Would he confidently affirm God's promises, or would doubt cloud his heart? In this act of faith, God provided a ram caught in the thicket, a perfect substitute for the sacrifice, embodying the essence of divine provision. Thus, we are reminded that true trust in God allows us to experience His Glory in remarkable ways, transforming our lives and those around us.

Abraham, a man of profound faith, believed in the promises of God, and this unwavering trust was credited to him as righteousness. The narrative unfolds further, revealing God's covenant with Abraham—a divine assurance to bless and multiply his descendants until they are as countless as the grains of sand on every shore, a testament to his obedience and faithfulness. In Genesis 22:15, a second call from heaven pierces the silence, the angel of the Lord declaring, "I swear by Myself, says the Lord, that because you have shown such faith and have not held back your only son, I will bless you abundantly. Your descendants will outnumber the stars in the heavens and the grains of sand on the sea. They will inherit the cities of their foes, and through your lineage, all nations on earth will be blessed, for you have followed my commands."

Obedience, my friends, unlocks the door to fulfillment in our lives. God is eagerly waiting for you to embrace this path of obedience. Just as He had prepared abundant blessings for Abraham, He is similarly preparing blessings for you, testing your readiness to receive what He has in store. In life, the pattern is clear: first comes the testing, then the blessing. God desires to see if you are equipped to manage the enormity of these blessings. Are you generous? Do you selflessly lend a hand to others in need? He seeks out those with giving hearts to bless abundantly. I recall a time when I aided my former church in moving an overwhelming number of potatoes across buildings; we employed large wheelbarrows to transport them all. My pastor's simple request remained etched in my mind: "Will you be obedient?" And that, dear friends, is precisely what God is asking of us today. "Will you be obedient?" The blessings are already prepared and waiting for you to embrace faith and stir up the talents within you for God's glory to shine through your life.

Like Abraham, when I accepted Christ as my Savior, my heart overflowed with indescribable joy. I was able to claim the blessings that God, in His foresight, had already laid out for me. Your blessings are indeed woven into the fabric of God's design; they are present in His thoughts long before you even conceive them. Yet, God remains patient, waiting for you to reach the level of maturity required to receive those gifts. If He were to grant them to you now, they might bear more harm than good simply because you're not ready to handle them. Just as God bestows a baby upon a mother at the perfect moment, knowing she is prepared to care for it, so too does He align His timing with your growth.

In 3 John 2, we find the words,

> “Beloved, I wish above all things that you may prosper and be in health, even as your soul prospers.”

God is profoundly interested in your well-being; He desires your health to flourish. This calls upon you to cherish your body, your divine temple, with good nourishment and honorable actions. You see, your body houses the Holy Spirit, and as He resides within, it becomes imperative to nurture your spiritual self. Pray diligently, and seek God's most profound desires for your life. After all, the scriptures remind us that God has a heart for your prosperity, but this requires you to remain in harmony with Him. Positioning yourself beneath God's loving authority is crucial. When you submit and insist on walking in His ways, His divine windows of Heaven will burst open, flooding you with blessings too grand to contain. True positioning is an exercise in humility, a practice of waiting, and therein lies tremendous power. To submit isn't merely to yield; it's an embrace of authority, a sacred alignment with a higher will. Under God's rule, there is no shame—only grace. He is a gentle shepherd, handling His children with a profound depth of compassion, nurturing their spirits as a gardener tends to his most precious blooms.

Consider the words from Matthew 9:36-37:

> "But when he saw the multitudes, he was moved with compassion on them because they fainted and were scattered abroad, as sheep having no shepherd. Then saith he unto his disciples, The harvest truly is plenteous, but the laborers are few."

These verses resonate deeply, for God's harvest is an abundance beyond measure. There is enough for every soul that seeks Him; jealousy and envy have no place in His kingdom. When God speaks of the few laborers, He does not lament a lack of harvest but a scarcity of those willing to toil in the fields of blessings.

Let us not confuse abundance with possessions; true greatness unfolds in our commitment to serve God and others. Do not flinch when labeled a "Jesus freak" or when critics hurl unkind words. For it is you, chosen by God, who finds authenticity and affirmation not in fleeting worldly accolades but in the divine truth of His love. The world offers glittering temptations that fade like morning mist, while God promises joys that stretch into eternity.

I reflect on my journey and recognize that had I settled for mediocre pleasures; I would not be the person I am today, radiating strength and purpose. As I walked hand in hand with God, savoring His presence and wisdom, doors began to swing open—opportunities to share His word and fulfill my calling. T.D. Jakes astutely remarked in his book "Destiny," "Destiny is the push of our instincts to the pull of our purpose." It is this innate instinct that propels us toward divine fulfillment.

When you feel the weight of despair as life's hurdles rise, remember to push through the resistance that seeks to hold you back. Whether confronting a job loss or heartache, redirect that energy into something meaningful and productive. During a particularly dark time in my life, I found solace in volunteering at a local homeless shelter serving warm meals to those in need. In the act of giving, I discovered healing—an essential truth that echoes in my spirit: when you extend love to others, God works within you. I am living proof that through service, there comes restoration.

Today, I stand healed, constantly striving to turn dreams into reality. Be discerning about whom you share your dreams with; not everyone is a cheerleader on your journey.

Some may embody the role of dream-killers, actively seeking to shatter your aspirations. Consider Joseph, who was favored by his father, who had a coat of many colors and was burdened with extraordinary visions. When he confided in his brothers, their response festered with hatred and resentment. In a world where many settle for the status quo, your ambitions may provoke disdain. Yet, do not be swayed; the fire that ignites your dreams burns brighter than any external persecution. Embrace the truth that what lies within you—your hopes, your faith, your purpose—is immeasurably greater than what the outside world perceives. Dare to dream and rise to fulfill your divine destiny.

You are of God, dear children, and you have triumphed over those trials that challenge your spirit, for the power that resides within you is far greater than any darkness that roams this world. Though hatred may permeate through the hearts of many, remember that the unique garment God has draped upon you signifies His immense favor. This favor is not fleeting; it is eternal! As Psalm 30:5 reminds us, His anger is but a moment's flicker while His favor shines brightly across a lifetime.

Reflecting on Joseph's story, he had no inkling that his brothers would choose betrayal. We can learn from this tale — Joseph embodied optimism and saw the world through a hopeful lens. His brothers, consumed with jealousy, failed to recognize their own blessings, leading to envy's bitter roots sprouting within them. It's not that others lack God's favor; rather, they often walk blinded to its presence in their lives, seeking fulfillment in gazing at another's gifts. Know this: Every time you rise with strength, Satan trembles, desperate to sidetrack you from your path of achieving your dreams.

The truth of the matter is that each morning, Joseph awoke, and he carried within him dreams that illuminated his destiny. My beloved friends, God is well able to bring your aspirations to fruition! Genesis 37:3 reveals how Israel cherished Joseph above all his children, for he was the beloved son of his elder years. In a gesture of love, he adorned Joseph with a vibrant coat, a symbol of his special place in the family.

Yet, the moment Joseph's brothers beheld their father's favoritism, they were consumed by hatred, unable to find solace in even a kind word towards him. This animosity only deepened when Joseph shared his dream—a vision of greatness that sparked jealousy anew.

In Genesis 37:9, we see Joseph dreaming yet again, unafraid to unveil his ambitions, revealing yet another divine message: "Behold, the sun, the moon, and the eleven stars bowed to me." His father, baffled and protective, scolded him for such a grandiose vision.

Sometimes, our nearest ones may struggle to support our lofty dreams, preferring for us to remain within the familiar and pursue paths of security rather than the uncertainty of true greatness. Yet, remember this: God has planted remarkable dreams within you! As you dare to remove all limits on God's power, He is eager to unleash blessings from the heavens above. When the outside world attempts to stifle your vision with its lack of understanding, do not allow fear to take root within.

For it is fear, when allowed to infiltrate, that can warp your emotions and cloud your judgment. You cannot walk with God while shackled by fear; refuse to be pushed into a corner by anyone. Just as Peter defied the raging waters to walk beside Jesus, recognize that your internal courage far outweighs external uncertainty. The God within you is infinitely more potent than what lies before you. Hold onto this truth: greatness resides in you, waiting to be unveiled to the world. Embrace it and walk forward with boldness.

Joseph, a spirit so trusting and pure, remained blissfully unaware of the darkness festering within his brothers. Even after they had allowed hatred to cloud their hearts, he ventured out into the fields, seeking his kin with an innocent hope. This act reflects a profound spiritual truth: that even in our ignorance when aligned with divine purpose, we remain vehicles for greater plans. For when you walk in faith, guided by God's invisible hand, you are destined to traverse the path laid before you, a path illuminated by promise. His father, Israel, called upon him, asking, "Are your brothers not tending their flocks in Shechem? Come, my son, I will send you to them." And with unwavering obedience, Joseph responded, "Here am I," earnestly embodying the spirit of willingness. Israel instructed him, “Go, find out how your brothers fare and the condition of the flocks; return with news.” Thus, with hope in his heart, Joseph departed from the vale of Hebron, the homeland he loved, and journeyed towards Shechem.

Along the way, a certain man, a stranger in the field, caught sight of him wandering and inquired, “What is it that you seek?” Joseph replied, “I am searching for my brothers. Please, direct me to where they tend their sheep.” The man provided the answer he sought: “They have moved on; I overheard them mention Dothan.” Without hesitation, Joseph pursued his brothers, determined to find them and spread harmony among them. Yet, as his figure appeared on the horizon, his brothers recognized him before he had drawn near and bitterness brewed among them—plotting against their own flesh and blood.

“Look! The dreamer approaches,” they murmured among themselves, eyes glinting with malice and envy. Their hearts plotted—“Let us slay him! We will cast him into a pit and claim a wild beast has devoured him. Then we shall witness what fate befalls his dreams.” The enemy delights in thwarting those who dare to dream, especially those brave enough to envision a greater destiny. Do not let fear silence the aspirations within you! Remember, cling to faith above fear, for within you lies an unconquerable spirit.

As we arrive at verse twenty-three, we observe a

pivotal moment: Joseph stripped of his coat, the vibrant symbol of his father's favor. Though the adversary may strip you of worldly possessions, they can never take the divine favor bestowed upon you. This alone is a cause for celebration! When he came to his brothers, they callously tore away his colorful coat, his identity stripped from him, and cast him into an empty pit, void of life and water. But this was not the end. From that pit, Joseph was carried away and sold into Egypt, where he served under Potiphar—his journey of training toward sovereignty had just begun.

Joseph discovered fulfillment through the very gifts God had entrusted to him. With a prophetic voice and the gift to interpret dreams, Joseph was a conduit for divine revelation. When Pharaoh, disturbed by his vivid dreams, sought understanding, it was through Joseph that God whispered the truth. Those who take the time may delve into Genesis 40 to uncover this miraculous narrative. Joseph's special gift was not merely for his own glory; it was a blessing to those around him, guiding them through their own dark moments.

Friends, remember this: what the devil intends for harm, God can intricately weave into a tapestry of good. Ultimately, Joseph ascended to greatness, becoming the steward of all of Egypt, a testament to the transformative power of faith and purpose.

Genesis 40:8 And Pharaoh inquired of his wise men, "Is there any man among us as remarkable as this? A man who possesses the Spirit of God?" 39 "Indeed, Joseph, since God has revealed the truths of the future to you, there is no one as wise and discerning as yourself," Pharaoh declared with conviction. 40 "From this moment forth, you shall have authority over my house, and by your command shall my people be guided; the only distinction shall be the throne before you." 41 With a gesture of finality, Pharaoh announced to Joseph, "You are now ruler over all the land of Egypt." 42 He removed his royal ring, placing it upon Joseph's hand, and adorned him in luxurious linen garments, fastening a golden chain around his neck as a symbol of his newfound authority. 43 Pharaoh commanded that Joseph ride in his second chariot, and to the astonishment of all, they proclaimed before him, "Bow the knee!" Thus, Joseph was appointed governor over all of Egypt's vast territories. 44 "I am Pharaoh," he proclaimed, "and in all this land, no man shall so much as lift a hand or a foot without your command."

This divine acknowledgment illustrates a profound truth: God has destined someone to recognize the spirit within you. Others may perceive the talents bestowed upon you by the Almighty, yet the critical question remains—will they act accordingly? It might take the most powerful of kings to elevate you to your rightful place, but take heart; transformation is on the horizon. The essence of this narrative teaches us to maintain tenacity in our dreams, for the Lord rewards those who persevere. Achieving fulfillment through God is the greatest pursuit one can undertake.

CHAPTER THREE

ALWAYS REMEMBER TO REJOICE

I often reflect on the power of perspective; even in moments of tribulation, I choose to smile in the face of my adversaries. God has elevated me above my enemies to such heights that their jeers and grievances become insignificant blips on my radar. This is where spiritual maturity unveils itself. One must possess the courage to overlook trivialities and let folly drift by like whispers in the wind. Gossip dances like an uninvited guest, lurking and spreading its contagion; if you linger too long in its vicinity, it will seep into your soul and dampen your spirit.

Feeling incapacitated and unable to rise from bed? Look closely; you may be burdened by the weight of the world's crises—concerns that were never intended for you to shoulder.

Remember, God is always there, particularly when circumstances paint a bleak picture or cast shadows of doubt on your self-worth and potential. Stand firm, look adversity in the eye, and proclaim the words of Philippians 4:13:

> I can do all things through Christ who strengthens me."

Cultivating a spirit of gratitude even amidst chaos transforms our outlook, filling our hearts with appreciation. To shift how you perceive others or the world around you, begin by nurturing appreciation. Thank God for the little things because these simple treasures mark the dawning of greatness. Zechariah 4:10 resonates here:

> For who has despised the day of small beginnings? They will rejoice and witness the plumb line in Zerubbabel's hand, for those seven signify the eyes of the Lord that roam throughout the earth."

God has a mysterious way of orchestrating the smallest elements of our daily lives in order to ignite extraordinary chain reactions. A single meeting can catapult you into a rewarding career, and a mere shift in your mindset could open the door to that long-desired promotion at work. Character, that often overlooked treasure, will propel you further than raw talent ever could. Consider the example of a talented NBA player—he can dazzle on the court, yet if he routinely tempers his passion with technical fouls, his brilliance risks being benched, overshadowed by his inability to master his emotional responses. It highlights an immutable truth: no matter how gifted you are if you fail to put a positive attitude at the forefront, you'll be stuck short of the divine greatness that God envisions for you.

Embrace every experience, even those that feel like

setbacks, because they are merely stepping stones in God's grand design for your life—a design aimed at crafting your impactful comeback. The further you're pulled back, like a tightly wound elastic band, the greater your potential launch.

I, too, prepared to write this book through extensive counseling and gleaning insights from many wise mentors. Learning to cultivate the right attitude during trials can significantly shorten the time it takes for God to guide you to the other side. The journey of the Israelites wandering the wilderness for forty long years serves as a poignant reminder of the consequences of a poor attitude. King Saul's rejection as king stemmed directly from his inability to maintain the right disposition.

Your attitude is a powerful determinant of your elevation in life. Even in the sacred role of parenthood, you must embody an attitude that serves as a guiding light for your children, teaching them how to navigate emotions and situations with grace. Avoid responding to life's challenges with negativity or bitterness, and refrain from casting blame on God. Allow His Word to penetrate the depths of your bitterness, paving the way for healing and renewal. You must consciously engage in the transformative practice of washing your mind with His Word each day. This renewal is vital; it aligns your thoughts with His purpose, echoing the biblical wisdom found in Romans 12:2, encouraging us not to conform to worldly patterns but to be transformed through the renewing of our minds, thereby discerning what is good and fulfilling in God's will.

Every time you open your heart to God's Word, you instigate the renewal of your mind. In this renewal lies your strength and freedom to step boldly into your divinely appointed destiny. Maintain an optimistic outlook. Cultivate gratitude in your heart for all of life's experiences, for indeed, all these things are working together intricately for your ultimate good, as echoed in Romans 8:28. Many set their sails toward their God-given destinies only to be anchored down by a faltering attitude.

Before I embraced my identity as a man of God, I had to undertake the challenging journey of realigning my mindset. Once, I believed the universe revolved around my whims and the dire need for my voice to carry the final word in every matter. My hubris was leading me to ruin. I lacked the solid foundation of Christ. His teachings remind us that anything constructed on unstable ground is doomed to collapse, yet a structure built on a firm foundation will stand resilient against the storms of life, as detailed in Matthew 7:24-27. The wise one, building on the rock, will withstand the torrents of rain and gale-force winds. In contrast, the foolish man grounded in shifting sand will falter, witnessing the great collapse of his efforts. Embrace this spiritual journey of renewal, fortify your stance on the rock, and watch as God guides you toward the horizon of your purpose, ready to transform your life and legacy.

The Bible declares with fervent clarity that without the sturdy foundation built on Christ, not only will you stumble—oh yes, you will fall, and your fall will be great. If I were occupying your shoes, I would gladly begin to rejoice and fortify myself with those things that endure the tests of time. Families can, indeed, thrive; marriages can experience profound restoration, and children can learn to honor their parents if only we collectively embrace the spirit of rejoicing. It's a common truth that a bitter attitude has the power to ruin an entire day, yet the armor of God stands as a formidable fortification along your journey. Each day, don that divine armor, for it empowers you to stand strong. Even when you have exhausted your efforts, your call is still to stand firm. Stand resolutely in the face of adversity; stand unyielding amidst scarcity, for this is your moment, your season, destined for blessings. Right now marks the perfect opportunity for you to align your attitude because the Lord's ears are wide open to your cries for help and guidance. Isaiah 40:28 challenges us:

> “Hast thou not known? Hast thou not heard that the everlasting God, the LORD, the Creator of the ends of the earth, fainteth not, neither is weary? There is no searching of his understanding."

The depths of God's understanding are beyond our reach, grander than we can fathom. His pathways are elevated above our own, so trust in Him to provide for your every need. There exists no fear in following the path of purpose, which beckons you to live with intention and passion. Strive for greatness, pour your heart into your endeavors, and give your all. To rejoice is to embrace love for God amid financial trials and marital strife. It is about finding happiness even when storms rage fiercely around you. Indeed, troubles do not last forever; God will carve a path through the chaos. We must take the time to correct our perspectives, adjusting our attitudes to welcome God into our thoughts. It may sound mundane, yet to have the Creator of the universe occupying your mind is a monumental gift. Remember, He desires for you to prosper and maintain good health.

Nurture your mind as diligently as you care for your body because a mind, dear brothers and sisters, is a treasure not to be squandered. Stand up from the couch, take initiative, and engage in actions that could transform your life. Start that business you've dreamed of, create a club that brings people together, volunteer in your community, and you will discover a profound sense of fulfillment. God has set you apart for a specific purpose.

The Bible assures us that you have been sanctified, meaning you are distinguished for a divine calling. Recall how the Lord revealed to Jeremiah that he was chosen from his youth, even though Jeremiah felt a heavy weight of fear confronting his calling. You, too, may feel apprehensive about the lofty call of God but press on nevertheless. Do you dare to step outside the comforting walls of your zone? When you choose to go forth in your fear, the shackles of that fear are broken from your life because you refuse to remain under its dominion. God knew you before your first breath and has a radical plan laid out for your life—so embrace it.

Then the word of the Lord came unto me, a voice resonating through the chambers of my heart, saying, "Before I formed thee in the belly, I knew thee; and before thou camest forth out of the womb, I sanctified thee, and ordained thee a prophet unto the nations." I responded, a tremor of doubt in my voice, "Ah, Lord God! Behold, I am but a child, unworthy of such a calling." Yet, the Lord reassured me, His words like a gentle wind, "Say not, I am a child: for thou shalt go to all that I shall send thee, and whatsoever I command thee, thou shalt speak." "Be not afraid of their faces," He declared, "for I am with thee to deliver thee."

In essence, He had you in mind. God, in His infinite wisdom, predestined each of us to an extraordinary purpose. Do not claim inadequacy, for greatness resides within you. You must cast away self-doubt and disregard the intimidating gazes of others. Whatever God has summoned you to undertake, you have the capability to achieve it! Trust in your inherent worthiness, for greatness is indeed inscribed deeply within your very being. As He meticulously crafted you, God knew the unique gifts He would embed within your spirit. He anticipated the moments you would falter, but remember, He is the God of the relentless rise.

I come today to extend a message of hope and renewal: Get back up again. Understand that there is a vast world beyond your immediate surroundings; there lies abundance, liberation, and divine purpose waiting for you. You must learn to envision existence not just within the physical realm but through a spiritual lens, allowing it to transform into tangible reality. Remove the shackles of limitation and the firm borders that hinder your potential so that God may release you from all that binds you.

At times, I find myself yearning to soar, propelled by the tremendous greatness nestled within my soul. It is imperative that you embrace your God-given talents and the authority that He has placed within your grasp.

Happiness, I have learned, is a deliberate choice; I stand firm in the belief that this truth guides us. Each day, I choose to awaken joyfully, counting the myriad of blessings that God lays before me. Indeed, we all possess room for growth and come to the realization that God's plans align with our best interests. No earthly love could even begin to rival the depth of His devotion. One of the many gifts of God is His wisdom in knowing when to say 'no.' Just as a parent may deny a child's every request for their ultimate welfare, so too does God guide us with love, knowing that not everything we desire is beneficial. We must comprehend that God's love is profound, unconditional, and everlasting; it does not waver based on our behavior. This transformative love envelops us, even in our frightened moments. God reassures us: "Through sickness and health, I will not forsake you."

When we celebrate in His presence, understand that your next blessing is waiting just around the corner. Always remember to express gratitude for the gifts you already possess, for God's abundance in your life hinges on your willingness to recognize the opportunities presented to you. Isaiah speaks truthfully, "If ye be willing and obedient, ye shall eat the good of the land." Indeed, the blessings of God are attached to our actions. When we commit to follow His path, we find fulfillment awaits us. To rejoice is to cultivate a heart of thankfulness, even for the minutiae of our existence. Every second of life, every skirmish fought, choose to embody gratitude. Even in the face of daunting circumstances – perhaps you find yourself out of work, unsure where your next meal will come from – remain thankful. This attitude of gratitude transforms our struggles into moments of growth and opens the door for God's boundless grace.

Elijah stood as a devoted prophet of the Lord, a steadfast messenger charged with the divine promise that sustenance would follow him relentlessly throughout his journey. In 1 Kings 17, the moment came when the word of the Lord pierced the silence of his thoughts, resounding with clarity and purpose: "Get thee hence, and turn thee eastward, and hide thyself by the brook Cherith, that is before Jordan."

Here, in this secluded haven, the Lord assured him that water would flow freely, and remarkably, He had commanded the ravens to deliver nourishment directly to him. Without hesitation, Elijah obeyed the divine instruction, journeying to the tranquil brook Cherith, nestled before the cradle of the Jordan. He settled there, enveloped by the serenity of nature. Each dawn, a pair of ravens brought him bread and meat, a miraculous testament to God's provision, not just once but twice a day, while the brook quenched his thirst. God's abundant provision was an affirmation of Elijah's faithfulness; he listened to the whisper of the Lord, a reminder that obedience opens doors to divine resources. But as life ebbed and flowed, Elijah learned that comfort can be a stagnating force. Just as he began to find solace in the daily rhythm of his surroundings, the narrative took another turn. After the blessed ravens had sustained him, God instructed him to journey onward. The divine plan unfolds in stages; God cherishes movement and growth, ensuring that His provision is not tied to a single location but flows wherever He sends you.

As the story continues, the word of the Lord flows again to Elijah: "Arise, go to Zarephath, which belongs to Sidon, and dwell there. Behold, I have commanded a widow there to feed you." Filled with purpose, Elijah set forth to Zarephath, a town that held the promise of new beginnings. Upon reaching the city gate, he spotted a widow diligently gathering sticks, her expression a blend of resolve and desperation. He approached her with a request for water, a simple yet vital necessity in such trying times. As she moved to fetch it, he called out, "And bring me a morsel of bread in your hand." The widow glanced back, her voice trembling as she replied, "As the Lord your God lives, I have nothing baked, only a handful of flour in a jar and a little oil in a jug. I am gathering sticks to prepare one final meal for my son; after that, we may face death."

In that moment of vulnerability, Elijah spoke words meant to penetrate fear: "Do not fear; go and do as you have said. But first, make me a little cake of it and bring it to me, and afterward, make something for yourself and your son. For thus says the Lord, the God of Israel, 'The jar of flour shall not be spent, nor the jug of oil become empty, until the day the Lord sends rain upon the earth.'" Emboldened by faith and an urgency to heed divine direction, she complied with his request. In this act of surrender, she and her household were blessed abundantly, eating from the miraculous supply that never diminished, fulfilling the Lord's promise spoken by Elijah.

Each day was marked by the wonder of God's provision, manifesting not just in physical sustenance but in the deeper awakening that trusting in His wisdom brings. The jar of flour remained steady, and the jug of oil never ran dry, all in accordance with the word of the Lord that echoed through Elijah's voice. In this way, the faithful journey of Elijah continued, reminding us that in surrendering to divine will, we open ourselves to infinite possibilities.

The widow, alone in her humble abode, faced the stark reality of her meager possessions—a paltry amount of meal and a few drops of oil, hardly enough to feed her beloved child. Nevertheless, a spark of hope flickered within her, igniting her willingness to act. She listened, truly listened, to the divine message delivered through the prophet. When God graces you with a directive, it carries weight beyond measure. His promises are the bedrock of faith, never falling short of their intended purpose.

In her moment of desperation, God instructed her to prioritize the needs of another before her own hunger, a test of faith that demanded sacrifice. With a heart full of trust, she obeyed, and as she shared what little she had, a miraculous truth unfolded—her supplies did not dwindle. This profound lesson resounded: when you generously offer yourself to others, God, in His infinite wisdom, will ensure your own needs are fulfilled. His abundance knows no bounds, flowing endlessly from His storehouse.

The crux of her experience was obedience—without it, one risks forfeiting the blessings that flow from divine favor. Consider Saul, who was commanded by the prophet Samuel to obliterate the Amalekite threat yet chose to spare both the king and the finest livestock. His disobedience spoke of selfish gain, and as a consequence, he shut the door on God's overflowing generosity.

As 1 Samuel recounts, Saul went forth to combat the Amalekites, eliminating those beneath the sword from Havilah to Shur, and indeed, he captured Agag. Still, instead of total destruction, he allowed greed to seep into his heart and linger among his people, leading them to hoard the best of the spoils, claiming piously that such offerings were destined for the Lord in Gilgal. But

Samuel, the obedient prophet burdened with the weight of Saul's transgressions, received a word from the Lord.

It was heavy, a sorrow that pierced his spirit, revealing that God's heart grieved over Saul's departure from His path. The prophet cried out through the night, a testament to his fidelity to the Lord. Saul, when confronted, feigned obedience, heralding his conquests yet failing to grasp his failures. "I have followed the Lord," he insisted, while truth lay cloaked in deception. His heart, ensnared by desire, could not see that true worship lay not in burnt offerings but in heartfelt adherence to God's commands.

Samuel's response illuminated the way: "To obey is better than sacrifice; hearing the Lord's voice is worth far more than any offering." In rebellion, Saul became akin to a sorcerer, stubbornness morphing into idolatry, and with each choice, he distanced himself from divine grace. Consequently, the lofty title of king was ripped away—an echo of the divine principle that rejection of God's word incites His withdrawal from our lives.

In this, we find a reminder that the journey of the spirit is paved not merely with intentions but with faithful adherence to divine guidance.

Rebellion is a grievous sin in the sight of the Lord, appearing as insidious as witchcraft itself. When God reflected upon His choice of Saul as king, His heart filled with remorse and regret due to Saul's disobedience—a clear signal of the consequences that accompany our choices. We must glean wisdom from Saul's narrative, recognizing that obedience is not merely a virtue but a pathway to divine blessings. It's always better to embrace the guidance of God and open ourselves to all the wonderful gifts He has in store than to play a risky game with disobedience.

In my youth, I turned a deaf ear to the wise counsel of those who cared for me, elders whose voices echoed with warnings like "Don't venture there" or "Avoid such deeds." My heart, hardened like stone, shut out their wisdom, reflecting the very struggle that Saul endured. My patterns of disobedience, regrettably, led to a diminishing of my place within the kingdom of God. Understand this: each of us possesses a sacred position within His realm, even if we lack titles like elder or pastor. In God's eyes, value is not conferred through titles but by the sincerity of our hearts and the readiness to serve.

I strongly urge you to seek a church home, for God always harbors a divine plan tailored for your life, interwoven with purpose and significance. The hours you might squander can instead be imbued with meaning—imagine joining a praise team, immersing yourself in fellowship, or even pursuing theological studies at seminary. Establish a connection in a local church community, commit to being present, and open your ears to the teachings of your pastor. Remember, true humility positions you to experience God's exaltation, just as 1 Peter 5:6-7 proclaims. Humble yourselves under the mighty hand of God, allowing Him to elevate you when the time is right.

Cast all your worries, your burdens, and your fears upon Him, for He genuinely cares about you and your struggles. He intimately understands your pain and emotions, sharing in your joy and heartache alike. It's essential to prioritize self-care and embrace the love that God extends toward you. Each moment, rejoice in the current season of your life; the next could unfold into the most beautiful chapter yet. In Chapter 5, we recognize this as God's process.

I have learned to endure all circumstances, hoping and believing through all trials, as echoed in 1 Corinthians 13. In the darkest hours, I have felt the gentle grip of God's hand, guiding me forward, ensuring that everything unfolds for my good. The journey may be fraught with difficulty, but I have cultivated the strength to endure. Endurance is the unwavering resolve to face unpleasant situations without yielding. Do not let setbacks define you; when one door closes, another opens.

I have faced numerous closed doors, but God, in His boundless grace, has swung open even larger avenues filled with promise. After all, He embodies the essence of abundance. Why not start vocalizing your trust in God? Forsake your reliance on your limited understanding and allow Him to chart your course. Trust the process, for as Psalm 37:23 assures us, the steps of a good man are ordered by the Lord, and he delights in His way.

Believe that the path God lays before you will be a source of joy, richer and sweeter than honey itself. Each step is an invitation to experience His divine favor, leading you toward a future infused with hope and fulfillment.

The journey may feel arduous at times, yet it blossoms into something more beautiful with each passing day. Our God is a fountain of compassion, extending His boundless mercy towards all His beloved children. When we reflect on our true worth, it's humbling to recognize what we truly deserve. Yes, it's a reality that without His grace, we all might find ourselves in the depths of despair. Yet, in His unfathomable love, God chooses to cradle us in His everlasting embrace.

I've come to deeply understand that God is gentle and nurturing; He cares for His children as a loving parent. He wants you to discover that within the grand design of creation, you are a uniquely divine piece carved out with intention—a piece that fits perfectly in a place only you can occupy. No matter how others may try to diminish your spirit or paint you in a foolish light, remember that what God has set aside for you is uniquely yours, unshakable by the opinions of the world.

We are all integral pieces in this magnificent puzzle called life, and it is crucial for you to allow God to unfold the beautiful purpose that awaits you. Take, for instance, T.D. Jakes—his journey to becoming Bishop was not a matter of happenstance; it was a labor of love and commitment, filled with study, planning, and strategic thinking. Similarly, Martin Luther King Jr. didn't rise to prominence as a civil rights leader overnight. He was meticulously shaped by God, crafted piece by piece, preparing him for the weighty responsibilities bestowed on him by divine providence.

Each of us has a purpose here on Earth, and upon discovering what that is, we will find profound satisfaction. As you navigate this path, take a moment to express gratitude for the mentors God has graciously placed in your life. Consider the strength of a great man —he does not arise isolated but rather on the shoulders of those who came before him. Each of us has drawn inspiration from others, mimicking their strength until we could flourish in our unique light.

I remember those days when I would leap

energetically in front of the mirror, channeling the presence of T.D. Jakes, envisioning myself preaching to countless souls. While that grand vision has yet to manifest, and I remain uncertain whether it aligns with God's will, what I am certain of is my commitment to relish the journey shaped by His hand.

Every reborn individual is akin to a finely tuned machine, invigorated by the powerful Word of God. This Word acts as a driving force, propelling you towards your true destiny. When you immerse yourself in the Scriptures with an open heart, ready to embrace their wisdom, the Word becomes interwoven with your very being. The benefits of this sacred text enrich your life profoundly. Your transformation cannot truly commence without engaging with the Word of God.

Like a skilled craftsman, the Word serves as a hammer, breaking through the hardest of hearts, softening them, and fostering a trust in your Creator that is unwavering and relentless. In light of Proverbs 3:5-6, "Trust in the LORD with all thine heart; and lean not unto thine own understanding. In all thy ways acknowledge him, and he shall direct thy paths," find solace in His unchanging hand.

It is vital to recognize that throughout this life's journey, pain may intertwine with joy. You may encounter rejection along the way, but the Bible reminds us to count ourselves blessed despite such trials. As noted in Matthew 5:11-12,

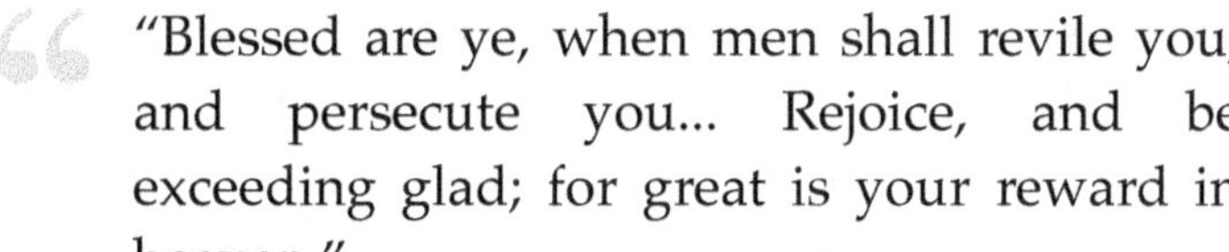

> "Blessed are ye, when men shall revile you, and persecute you... Rejoice, and be exceeding glad; for great is your reward in heaven."

Find someone who resonates with your spirit, someone who can walk alongside you through this transformative journey. You cannot traverse this path of life alone, for it demands the warmth and support of a steadfast companion. Seek out a prayer warrior, a brave soul unafraid to confront the shadows and rebuke the devil with fervor.

I was fortunate to grow up among individuals who exuded courage in the face of spiritual warfare; I never hesitated to approach the altar, believing wholeheartedly in God's healing grace. Fear should never serve as a barrier to receiving God's abundant blessings. Although some may cast sideways glances or whisper unsavory remarks, remain steadfast and keep forging ahead. There exists a higher calling upon your life—a divine purpose that sets you apart. Many are called to embark on this journey, yet few are chosen to fulfill their destinies. Jesus spoke of this truth, understanding that not everyone would choose to submit to His divine authority.

As we find in 2 Timothy 2:3-5, we are encouraged: "Thou therefore endure hardness, as a good soldier of Jesus Christ." To be a soldier for Him requires resilience and the ability to stay unentangled from the trivial pursuits of this world, focusing instead on pleasing Him who has enlisted us. Your focus must remain solely on divine love, not being ensnared by the fleeting pleasures this life offers. After all, the joys of this world are temporary; God's provisions, however, are of everlasting substance.

You must endure, for a glorious calling awaits you, and God is still working within you. If you find yourself still being shaped and molded by His love, stay steadfast in your position; God's best is reserved for those who seek Him earnestly—the key to unlocking God's best lies in your obedience. When you learn to rejoice and follow His commandments, the Spirit of God will guide you along the purpose-filled path He has laid out for you.

Simply put, listen to the soft whisper of His voice rather than the clamor of your flesh. Remember, the flesh does not lead to a heavenly destiny; it returns to dust, where it belongs. Therefore, triumph over the flesh and its worldly desires. As Galatians 5:17-18 notes, "For the flesh lusteth against the Spirit, and the Spirit against the flesh." These opposing forces can create turmoil within, making it challenging to align with God's will. Yet, if you yield to the Spirit, you free yourself from the constraints of the law, which demands righteousness through rigid rules.

God proclaims your righteousness stems simply from walking in alignment with Christ. Christ stands as your mediator, much like a fervent advocate in a courtroom, interceding for your right to worship and praise the Almighty. Do not let anything quench your praise; the destination God has planned for you transcends human imagination. He desires to lead you to lands flowing with milk and honey, promises that are rich and overflowing.

Consider the journey of the children of Israel—they wandered for years as a result of their complaints about sustenance, idols, and timing. You must remain conscious of the divine timing, which is never akin to our temporal perspectives. God's timing is flawlessly orchestrated, and He knows precisely when to unveil your blessings. The Bible reminds us to wait unwaveringly upon the Lord and to embody courage in our hearts. Courage is not merely a concept; it is a demonstration of faith amidst adversity. It shows God that you are prepared to walk faithfully with Him.

With courage as your armor, you position yourself to receive the abundance of God's greatest blessings. Just as David summoned remarkable courage before Goliath and Samuel displayed the same when anointing him, you, too, can embody courage through your faithful obedience to God's word. Stand strong; your journey has only just begun.

Obedience, at its very core, is a profound journey of sacrifice and understanding. It begs the question: what are you truly willing to relinquish so that God can manifest His divine purpose in your life? Reflect on the distractions we often cling to—some of which we might realize, upon deeper scrutiny, are entirely unnecessary.

I made a pivotal decision to relinquish secular music, a choice that opened pathways to a deeper, more intimate walk with God, and because of that, I feel His presence more closely than ever before. I chose to cast aside the fleeting pleasures of this world to embrace the eternal comfort of Christ. When life's workings feel bewildering, and you find yourself at a crossroads, I urge you—to hold fast to Christ. In moments when blessings seem just out of reach, when hope appears faded, cling tenaciously to Him. When the judgments of the world weigh heavy on your heart, rely on the steadfast hand of God, which remains unchanged through every storm we face.

Understanding this process is an essential step in our spiritual growth; it becomes a lesson in humility and resilience. The Apostle Paul, in his moment of vulnerability, cried out to the Lord, beseeching Him to remove the thorn that plagued his flesh. Yet God responded not with removal but with a gentle reassurance, "My grace is sufficient for you." Paul realized that in his moments of weakness, when he felt most powerless, God's strength would rise to meet him, illuminating the path forward.

Just as Paul recognized the gift of his afflictions, so too should we learn to embrace our struggles as opportunities for growth. "And lest I should be exalted above measure through the abundance of revelations," Paul wrote, "there was given to me a thorn in the flesh, the messenger of Satan to buffet me." He sought relief from this burden three times, only to be reminded that the very weakness that troubled him was a canvas for divine strength.

God's strength—precisely calibrated for our moments of doubt and fear—serves as our sanctuary. He is the strong tower into which we flee, the fortress that shields us from life's uncertainties and the rock upon which we can confidently stand. Like Paul, let us embrace our vulnerabilities, for it is within them that God's power thrives. I find solace in my own gentle spirit and vulnerability, unafraid to let my heart remain open, knowing that God guards it closely, nurturing it with His unwavering love.

Let us exuberantly glorify God's power, recognizing His ability to protect and present us as blameless before the world. Thanks to the unmerited favor bestowed upon us through the sacrifice of Christ on the cross, we are liberated to bask in His grace. As it is written in Hebrews 4:16, "Let us therefore come boldly unto the throne of grace, that we may obtain mercy, and find grace to help in time of need." Approach His throne without trepidation; God does not judge our imperfections. Instead, He transforms our weaknesses into testimonies of His glory.

Even in areas where you may feel inadequate—perhaps public speaking isn't your forte, or maybe sports are a realm in which you don't shine—rest assured that God's grace will envelop you. No matter your abilities or perceived shortcomings, His grace has the power to cover every facet of your life. Grace, in its purest form, represents an undeserved favor that God lavishes upon us as His beloved children. Unlike the conditional favor of man, which often hinges on performance or achievement, divine love forgives effortlessly and abundantly.

It is the kind of love that overlooks transgressions countless times, not allowing anyone to fall beyond redemption. God doesn't operate on a strike-three basis. No, He embodies the essence of mercy and forgiveness. It is this understanding that empowers us to extend grace to others, cultivating a world where love prevails over judgment.

As we navigate our lives, let us remember that obedience is not merely about following rules; it is about surrendering our hearts and lives to God's transformative power. Let us be willing to let go of what holds us back, trusting that in our obedience, we will discover the abundant life He has promised. Embrace the journey, knowing that every step taken in faith brings us closer to the divine purpose that awaits us.

"Forgiveness is not merely a transaction grounded in the sincerity of an apology or an attempt at reconciliation; it stems from a deep-seated love for God and a commitment to follow His divine guidance. True forgiveness is an act of devotion that transcends the need for reciprocation. Even if the individual who has wronged you chooses not to extend their own forgiveness, embracing forgiveness releases you from the shackles of resentment and bitterness that can otherwise bind your spirit.

Imagine unforgiveness as butane in a lighter—when ignited, it has the potential to unleash a consuming flame that can engulf your very being. This consuming fire is bitterness, and it can poison your relationships, cloud your thoughts, and drain your joy. When you harbor bitterness, it becomes nearly impossible to coexist peacefully with those you grudgingly hold in contempt. Your heart is devoid of tranquility; instead, you're caught up in a relentless cycle of thoughts centered on how to see the other suffer, mirroring your own pain. Yet amidst this turmoil, God gently beckons, "Let it go."

There is profound strength to be found in the act of forgiveness. The scriptures remind us of the weight of this responsibility: if we do not forgive others, we should not expect our own forgiveness from God, as stated in Mark 11:26: "But if ye do not forgive, neither will your Father which is in heaven forgive your trespasses." Forgiveness is not just a noble act; it is a divine command that can lead to your liberation.

So, take that step—release yourself from the chains of unforgiveness. Embrace the freedom to live your life to its fullest potential, unencumbered by past grievances. This freedom allows you to pursue your dreams and aspirations without hindrance. After all, why should you envy another's journey when the Creator of blessings is by your side? Everything remains firmly in God's hands, and believing this truth empowers you to embark on your best life.

When envy seeps into your heart, you may find yourself longing for what others possess, convinced they live lives untouched by struggle. Yet, the reality is that you are unaware of the many tears they have shed on their path to success. Perhaps they occupy the role of a thriving business owner or a CEO, but understand that if you match their effort and dedication, you too can attain similar achievements. The gifts and talents God has bestowed upon you are as significant as those given to anyone else. Remember, God has not overlooked you.

Take a moment to express your gratitude for the blessings already present in your life. This simple act can fundamentally alter your perspective. You will discover an abundance of joy and an ocean of peace. Gradually, an attitude of gratitude blossoms within you, and God's work in your life accelerates. However, recognize that God's process is rarely swift; it demands patience and steadfast discipline to guide you toward the destiny He has prepared for you. Ultimately, your attitude plays a crucial role.

It communicates to God your true desire for blessings. A positive, uplifting attitude can carry you further than any degree or accolade ever could. The scriptures also reveal that a good reputation holds far greater value than material wealth, emphasizing this truth in Proverbs 22: "A good name is rather to be chosen than great riches, and loving favor rather than silver and gold." Embrace this understanding, and let it guide you toward a life of purpose and fulfillment.

In this journey of obedience, forgiveness, and growth, remember that each step taken toward grace and gratitude brings you closer to the abundant life God has designed just for you. Trust in His timing, remain steadfast in your faith and allow the transformative power of love and forgiveness to shape your heart and guide your steps. You are on a path paved with divine purpose, and every act of faith unlocks new doors of possibility in your life. Embrace it fully."

"Favor" is a powerful force, a divine whisper that can usher us into places we never thought possible. It can manifest a new job, a shiny car, or an opportunity that seems beyond our reach. The grace of God is something we do not inherently deserve, yet, in His infinite love, He generously bestows it upon us.

I can recall the pivotal year of 2015—unexpectedly, favor propelled me into a position I felt utterly unqualified for. That year, I embraced the role of student governor of our university's student government association, and it was nothing short of transformative. Through this role, I was able to lift countless students as I walked confidently in my own path, a testament to the collective journey we share. There was a remarkable joy that came with serving others, an exhilaration in helping my fellow classmates achieve their aspirations.

I held steadfast dreams in my heart—dreams that God was beautifully orchestrating, ready to fulfill in His majestic timing. He truly is the God of dreams, poised and eager to transform those dreams into reality. Reflecting on favor, it transcends mere social media acknowledgments, like a thumbs-up or a shared post. It is magnificent, a profound gift granted when we step into obedience to God.

Through humility, doors swung open for me in ways I could never envision—like finding my picture featured on the school website, a blessing I never even sought. Such is the majestic work of God; He meets us at the intersection of our unqualified state and the fulfillment of extraordinary destinies, urging us to recognize that we all carry greatness within us, waiting to be unlocked with His guiding hand.

As I chase my own dreams—to become a best-selling author, to own a hotel bustling with laughter and life where conferences and celebrations unfold—I hold fast to this belief: no dream is considered less valuable in the eyes of God. Every aspiration holds weight in His kingdom, all within reach with diligence and gratitude. It's essential to cultivate thankfulness for even the tiniest blessings God imparts, for every seed planted in faith has the potential to grow into a magnificent tree bearing rich fruit.

When God declared to Adam, "Be fruitful and multiply," He commissioned him to embrace his destiny, to live fully into his purpose. Adam's calling was monumental—he became the father of generations, thriving in his role. This provokes a pivotal question for each of us: What is your purpose? What unique calling beats within you? It all begins with recognizing your identity as a cherished child of the Most High, and I pen these words to remind you of your infinite potential.

The gifts and talents you possess lie dormant within, yet they await the gentle touch of the Divine to be cultivated and harnessed for the advancement of His kingdom. Every intrinsic gift bestowed by God is intended to edify, uplift, and bless those around us. As we engage with our unique offerings, let us strive to fulfill the directive in Colossians 3:23: “And whatsoever ye do do it heartily, as to the Lord, and not unto man.” This beautiful passage challenges us to direct our gifts back towards Him, utilizing them solely for His glory rather than personal fame or accolades.

Know this: When God endowed you with your gifts, He foresaw your purpose, fully aware that your journey would involve trials. Yet, He equipped you with tools and treasures to navigate the paths you will traverse. It is crucial to dedicate your life to uncovering the profound reasons behind your existence, understanding that He has placed a significant calling upon your heart. This calling invites you into a dance of glorifying Him in all your endeavors.

When your purpose aligns harmoniously with His pleasure, expect a cascade of blessings beyond your wildest dreams. God is indeed my hero. His loving presence rescued me in times of uncertainty, illuminating the way when darkness clouded my vision, and for that, I remain forever grateful.

As you reflect on your own journey, remember that favor is not just for a select few; it is available to all who seek God earnestly. Embrace the opportunities He places before you, and trust that as you walk in obedience, His favor will guide you to places you never imagined possible. Each step you take in faith is a testament to His goodness, and every dream you hold dear is a reminder of His limitless grace. So, step boldly into your calling, knowing that God's favor will accompany you every step of the way.

When I found myself at the lowest point of my existence, it was He who reached for me, cradling my shattered spirit. He is the beacon of light that has guided me back, the very reason I breathe the air of this beautiful life today. For those of you seeking solace, I implore you to keep God at the forefront of your journey.

When God is first in your life, He will weave a tapestry of provision that encompasses every aspect of your being.

It's a profound truth: when you choose to prioritize Him, you'll discover that all your needs are not only met but also transformed into blessings. In this divine alignment, every twist and turn, even the setbacks you encounter, are but stepping stones in preparing your path for God's greater purpose in your life. I remember the haunting days of my past, filled with mistakes and uncertainty, often questioning, "Where is God in all this chaos?" But in those moments of despair, God was ever so close, tenderly clasping my hand, assuring me I was never alone.

Each breath we take is a testament to His presence, and every step we take is a dance of glory in His name. God delights in your success, sharing the weight of your failures and feeling the sting of your disappointment alongside you. He is intimately aware of your struggles because, in His infinite wisdom, He experiences life through your eyes and heart.

I speak directly to the hurt and pain that nestle within you, even the wounds of rejection that ache so deeply. Know this: God is always there to mend your heart. The key lies solely in your willingness to surrender your burdens to Him. How can you expect Him to know your heart if you remain silent? Let your honesty flow—share every detail of your pain with Him. "Today, someone hurt me, and I feel anger swell within me. Lord, I wish to retaliate, but I know this is not right. So, Lord, I ask You to take away these feelings."

It is essential that you address your true emotions before you can truly open your heart to God. God is fully aware of your feelings and knows every secret you harbor deeply within. His ear is inclined toward your cries—listen closely for His gentle voice. While He might be breaking you down, remember He is simultaneously reshaping you into His masterpiece. Just like beautiful pottery emerges from seemingly useless mud, you too can be formed into something extraordinary in the hands of the Master Potter.

To truly be molded by God, you must willingly submit to His transformative process. I recall a heartfelt conversation with my mother at our dinner table, where she vividly spoke about the trials of God shaping our lives. I remarked, "You know, the real issue is that we don't remain on the potter's wheel, do we?" She nodded, realizing the wisdom in my words. As God's children, it is imperative that we position ourselves where He can continue to mold and craft us. We must remain pliable, ready to be shaped, even when that means enduring a messy process.

Each step you take, and every challenge you face is a crucial part of your divine journey. Allow Him to finish the work He has begun in you, and in retrospect, you will witness the magnificent manifestation of His glory woven throughout your life's tapestry.

I once wrote a poignant poem that I carry in my heart: "Life, life, beautiful life, I'm pressing on past the strife, beyond the wicked, and the whispers of doubt, soaring high like a mighty hawk." It is vital to rise above negativity and refuse to let it obscure your destined path. There exists but one destiny uniquely crafted for you, waiting for you and God to step boldly into it together.

Give God glory in every triumph and trial, for He is the master craftsman who makes all things beautifully new. Remember, your journey is not in vain; every moment of struggle is a brushstroke in the masterpiece that is your life. Trust in His process, lean into His love, and allow the beauty of His handiwork to unfold in ways you have yet to imagine. Keep your heart open and your spirit willing, for God is always at work, crafting a story of hope, redemption, and divine purpose just for you.

This life, my friends, is a profound journey not just of receiving but of giving, a sacred exchange that echoes throughout the scriptures. The Bible recounts countless moments when individuals chose to give sacrificially before they ever experienced the bountiful rewards of receiving. Take Joseph, for instance; he served under Potiphar, enduring trials and tests, even finding himself confined behind bars before his dreams materialized into reality. Sometimes, in our own quests, we must traverse through our personal hells, often for injustices that we had no part in creating.

I've been labeled a bit eccentric—sometimes even deemed "crazy"—for my glimpses of the divine, for perceiving angels that others dismiss. Yet, had I allowed the futile whispers and judgment of the world to deter me, I would not stand here transformed into the man I am today. If I had succumbed to the shadows of negativity, I, too, would be ensnared in defeat. Delight yourself, my dear friend, in the abundant things of God, and He, in His infinite generosity, will grant you the deepest desires of your heart. He is poised, waiting, eager to shower you with blessings, but it requires your willingness to position yourself to receive.

I fully comprehend that the road can be riddled with challenges, including the scars of past abuses. However, it is imperative to don a fresh pair of eyes. Embrace the vision that comes from the living Word of God. The Bible reassures us that we are fearfully and wonderfully made. Every single one of us—crafted with purpose—has been purchased at a price immeasurable, far exceeding silver and gold. You ought to embrace life's beauty and pursue your best existence while breath fills your lungs, for it's never too late to step into the fullness of what God has in store for you. Open your heart and receive abundantly now, for complacency can rear its head if we wait too long. Expect more from your life; avoid becoming comfortable in mediocrity. Strive for the grander vision, continually acknowledging that all glory belongs to God alone.

When Scripture instructs us to do all things in His name, it implores us to keep Him at the forefront of our every action. People might overlook the beauty in your endeavors, but rest assured, God sees every act of kindness and every effort made in His honor. He is the author and finisher of our faith. What He begins, He brings to completion. Just like a writer revising their draft, God lovingly revises your life story, weaving miracles into your narrative, often behind the scenes.

This is why praise holds monumental importance in our lives. Even in times of weariness, praise Him fervently. Offer Him radical praises that resonate through the heavens. Those who stand on the sidelines may not grasp your reasons, but they are only witnessing part of the story—God's divine deliverance in your life and soul. You might have once walked the roads of a gangster, battled the chains of addiction, or faced your own storms of identity—but know this: God loves you precisely as you are. Your praise becomes a potent weapon, propelling darkness away. Each utterance of praise sends the enemy fleeing. When I lift my voice, demons scatter in fear, for Satan cannot fathom how one so overwhelmed could still resonate gratitude and joy. He ponders, "How can he glorify God amidst all that turmoil? How could she maintain her joy?"

The truth is, our praises spring not solely from what God is doing right now but from the ocean of grace and goodness He has already poured into our lives! Let your spirit erupt with praise! Each act of worship is a shattering of chains, an obliteration of shackles. When you pour out your heart in praise, God responds, weaving threads of salvation for lost loved ones into the fabric of your prayers. Remember, God's heart aches for no one to perish. So go forth, praise Him as though every prayer is already answered, for in the realm of faith, it is indeed done.

Beloved, do not overlook this crucial truth; there exists a divine perspective that transcends human understanding. One day in the presence of the Lord is akin to a thousand years, and a thousand years seem like just a fleeting day. This insight reveals that God, in His infinite wisdom, is already working in your tomorrow, orchestrating plans for prosperity and purpose in your life. Life often presents us with tests of obedience, reminders that we must return to a posture of humility before God.

Embrace this truth: God sees you through the challenges and wants you to know that His love for you is extraordinary, unique, and unwavering. Scripture reminds us that His desire is for us to flourish and be in good health, reflecting the well-being of our souls. The manner in which we respond to God's discipline shapes our potential for blessings; it is a choice we must consciously make. Consider the concept of unmerited favor—God bestows it upon us without conditions, regardless of what we think we deserve. He says, "This is my beloved child, and no force can diminish my blessing from them."

Understand that every event in life carries significance. Though it may not make sense at the moment, as time unfolds, clarity will come, unveiling the true essence of existence. Life may not consistently present you with challenges you can easily manage, but learn to turn every trial into a source of strength, just as you would make lemonade from lemons. Remember the wisdom found in James: count it all joy when you encounter various trials, for these tests refine your faith and cultivate patience. God desires for you to develop endurance and resilience; His intentions are not punitive but formative.

Without the firm hand of discipline, where would we be today? Just as a loving father chastises his children to cultivate growth and strength, so too does our Heavenly Father. It is through His guidance that I have grown and matured. The adversities that the enemy intends for our downfall are transformed by God into instruments for good. Every challenge, every hardship, no matter how overwhelming it appears—like endless bills pressing in —will ultimately lead to resolution.

You have yet to experience your fullest potential; the best that God has in store for you is still forthcoming. His blessings are abundant and overflowing. At times, you may feel disheartened, questioning why progress seems stagnant. In these moments, remember God is preparing you for the remarkable blessings ahead. The journey toward abundant grace often walks through valleys of suffering. As Jesus taught, if we endure hardship alongside Him, we will also share in His glory.

You might ask yourself, "Why am I feeling rejected by others? Why do I often seem an outsider? Why does my path feel burdened with trials?" Take heart, for these challenges are purposeful—a divine shaping for your good. Whatever you are experiencing, embrace it with joy; wear a smile that shines through adversity. Let not the trials of the world dampen your spirit. Stand tall, courageous and strong, for God stands firmly by your side.

Your journey may feel prolonged, but this is a testament to the greatness of the blessing awaiting you. A door of opportunity is being prepared, one so magnificent it can only be opened with patience. Lift your countenance, and let the joy of God's love radiate from you. Do not allow the world to diminish your smile —shine brightly, letting all see the light of a heart devoted to a mighty God.

After the trials and tribulations of life have tested your spirit, there comes a time when God will usher in His glory upon you. He understands the weight of your suffering, and He wants you to rest assured that each hardship is weaving a tapestry for your good. God moves in His own time, and indeed, timing is the ultimate key. As the magnificent heavens and the earth were meticulously crafted over time, so too will He patiently orchestrate the life you aspire to live.

Our goal should be to cultivate a life steeped in discipline and righteousness, reflecting the essence of Jesus Christ in our every action. Even in His darkest hour, when Christ faced the unbearable agony of crucifixion, He chose silence over retaliation, enduring the pain with steadfast grace. We, too, must grasp the art of endurance. Though the path may sting, God has imbued every hurt with purpose. These trials are not merely obstacles; they are shaping stones, honing our character and resilience as we learn to walk closely with God.

As I ventured deeper into my spiritual walk, I gleaned invaluable insights about character. A man's character is his true essence—shaped by his choices and the lens through which he views right and wrong. To earn God's favor, we must cultivate a character that mirrors His virtues. This walk involves respecting Divine commands and treating our fellow beings with honor and consideration. Character fundamentally revolves around the impression you leave on others. Are you living as a beacon of kindness and respect, or do you exude negativity and grumpiness? God evaluates us based on the fabric of our character, urging us to instill the right attitude amidst our interactions, instilling respect for parents among our youth.

Character can serve as a bridge to opportunities that mere degrees cannot cross. Look at Joseph, whose unwavering integrity earned him rulership over Potiphar's house, or David, whose noble character led him to the throne. It always circles back to your attitude. Do you often wear a smile, offering gratitude for the dawning of each new day? It takes discipline to maintain this attitude of thankfulness—a crucial tenet of a life well-lived. If God asserts that a good name holds more value than riches, then no amount of wealth can usurp the power of character. Good character can elevate you to the helm of a Fortune 500 company in mere years, can lead you to head a praise team at church, and can open the floodgates of divine blessing.

Embodying the right character means displaying serenity and radiating God's love for all to behold. We are empowered to live as testimonies of His magnificent acts on this earth. In this role, we embody the spiritual representations of God's glory, as God has woven humanity into His divine narrative. Every assignment He has given us seems grand, perhaps beyond our grasp, but we must hold fast to the truth that God's grace is inexhaustibly sufficient. His unmerited favor will carry you through the winding paths of life, just as the resilience of your character will nurture your journey.

He promises to never burden you beyond what you can endure, reminding us in 1 Corinthians 10:13 that temptations may arise, but God remains faithful. He will provide you with a way to escape each trial, ensuring you have the strength to bear it. Remember, whatever challenges confront your spirit, they are not solitary. Others have walked this path before you, bearing burdens that echo your own. Cling to this truth and let it buoy your spirit in times of distress.

You can celebrate with a joyous heart right now, for the burdens you bear are not too heavy for God to handle. Instead of magnifying your troubles, start proclaiming the vastness of your God to your challenges. That shift in perspective can transform everything! Your problems are merely insignificant ripples in the ocean of His might. As the Sovereign Creator of the universe, He cradles the world as effortlessly as a parent holds a child. The Bible assures us of His omnipotence; He is the ultimate source of power, and we trust that He is fully capable of navigating you through your struggles.

Always remember to embrace joy, even in the midst of trials and tribulations. God's promises resonate with an unwavering "yes" and "amen." They are steadfast, as He cannot deviate from His divine word. As Psalm 119:105 declares, "Thy word is a lamp unto my feet and a light unto my path." His word serves as your compass, illuminating the way through life's darkest valleys. If you've traversed the heart-wrenching journey of a divorce, just as I have, you will witness the splendor of His glory manifested through His teachings. Those sacred words will produce tangible, transformative results in your life, which is why I treasure them so deeply.

During times of solitude, it has been His word that embraced me and kept me steady. In the quiet hours of the night, He wrapped me in His comforting presence. He welcomed me with arms wide open, granting me liberation from guilt and the snares of this world. The word, firmly anchored in your heart, can work miracles. It has the power to lift you from anguish, dissolve your stresses, and shine as a beacon of hope at the end of the darkness. Remember, He will never impose upon you more than you can bear!

Though hell may unleash its mightiest foes against you, if you stand firm against the devil's schemes, your resilience will render his plans fruitless. The Bible cautions us that our struggles are not against mere mortals; rather, we wrestle against unseen forces of darkness and spiritual wickedness that lurk in high places. Ephesians reminds us to relinquish the temptation to fight with one another and instead allow the Lord to battle for us. In Ephesians 6:12, we read, "For we wrestle not against flesh and blood, but against principalities, against powers, against the rulers of the darkness of this world, against spiritual wickedness in high places."

Furthermore, the scriptures instruct us to don the full armor of God to stand strong against adversity. The first piece is the helmet of salvation, safeguarding our minds against the senseless assaults of the enemy. Ephesians 6:13-17 exhorts us: "Wherefore take unto you the whole armour of God, that ye may be able to withstand in the evil day, and having done all, to stand." So, stand tall with your loins girded in truth, your chest protected by the breastplate of righteousness, and your feet ready with the gospel of peace. Above all, wield the shield of faith, which will extinguish every fiery dart from the wicked one. Lastly, take the helmet of salvation and grasp the sword of the Spirit—it is the word of God itself that will empower and uplift you on your journey.

Your loins, girded with the unshakable truth of God's word, serve as a formidable shield against any physical adversities you may face. This divine truth does not merely protect your body; it illuminates your path, guiding you toward the right decisions at every crossroad of life. Wear proudly the breastplate of righteousness—it's more than an adornment; it signifies your rightful standing with God. Embrace the weight of forgiveness, knowing that your sins are washed away, allowing you to stand tall in His presence.

Always be prepared to share the gospel, for the act of spreading His word is an enduring testament of faith. Moreover, the shield of faith stands resolute, blocking the fiery darts of the enemy, fortifying your soul and spirit against his relentless attacks. But understand this: the mightiest weapon you possess is the sword of the Spirit, which is the word of God. It is this sacred scripture that unveils the profound truth about your identity. Too many people find themselves shackled by the weight of ignorance, unaware that the God who dwells within them is far greater than any challenge they may encounter.

As God's chosen people, we must don His armor each day, readying ourselves for the battles ahead if we wish to thrive in this life. Although God's process may test our resolve and push us to our limits, He assures us that emerging from these trials will leave us pure and sinless, as affirmed in Job 23:10:

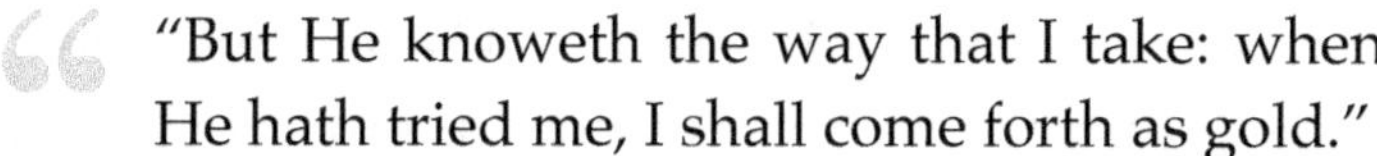

> "But He knoweth the way that I take: when He hath tried me, I shall come forth as gold."

CHAPTER FOUR
GET YOUR PRAISE ON

Praise is more than mere words; it is an expression of deep-seated admiration and warm approval. In times of struggle, God calls on His faithful to lift their voices in praise, transcending their circumstances. I vividly recall the Sundays from my childhood when I was enveloped in the joyful cacophony of the choir. My hands danced in rhythm, and my feet stomped in unison as we gathered around the pulpit, united in our devotion to God. It was in those moments that I realized my praise was a spiritual weapon, a powerful countermeasure against the enemy's relentless schemes. Here's what praise can do for you: it will be your fortress of strength. When despair looms like a shadow over your heart, lift your voice in adoration. Show Him your love and gratitude, and let your worship be an offering to the Almighty.

In those moments of praise, while you glorify God, He will impart strength to your weary soul, empowering you to continue the fight. Remember, your true strength isn't gauged by muscle or might; it's revealed in your unwavering praise during life's most challenging seasons. Your praises resonate the loudest when you find yourself in the darkest of hours, acting as a beacon of faith that pleases God. A spontaneous praise break can send the enemy retreating in disarray. Not only will it uplift your spirit, but it will also reverberate through your family and community, fortifying your children, your spouse, and your church family. So, praise God fervently for everyone you cherish, and witness how His grace creates ripples of deliverance in their lives.

As Psalm 33:1 reminds us,

> Rejoice in the LORD, O ye righteous: for praise is comely for the upright."

It is entirely natural to lift your voice in praise, especially in the throes of adversity. Praise draws you closer to God, building a sacred bridge between you and the Creator. When you draw near to Him, He wholeheartedly reciprocates. Moreover, praise calms the turbulence of the human experience. We tend to fret over trivial matters, but honoring God amidst trials will usher in a profound peace. During my tumultuous divorce, it was my praise that granted me the serenity to wait on God's timing, leaving me whole and restored in the end.

You may find it puzzling why such trials cross your path, but take solace in the wisdom of David, who proclaimed in Psalm 34:1, "I will bless the Lord at all times; His praise shall continually be in my mouth." Regardless of the storms you weather, guard your praise fiercely—it is the key that unlocks the divine for your benefit. When your heart overflows with gratitude and adoration, you invite God's hand to work wonders in your life. Do not hold back; this is not the time to mute your song of praise, for it is in this sacred season that miracles abound.

Moreover, praise serves as a bridge into communion with the Almighty. It is the divine language that echoes joy through the heavens. God's heart swells with happiness as we honor Him with our voices. We were created for this very purpose—to magnify His name in worship. He endowed us with the gift of music, a sweet symphony that allows us to revel in His presence. So, if your spirit yearns to draw nearer to Him, lift your voice—let a shout of joy burst forth, or a song of love escape your lips, and you will witness God move in your midst, responding to your heartfelt expression.

Even the angels, resplendent in their heavenly choir, sing, "Holy, Holy, Holy." Everything in creation is designed to reverberate with praise. The Scriptures remind us that if we remain silent, the very stones will rise up in worship! As the multitude gathered, rejoicing and lifting their voices in praise at the descent of the Mount of Olives, they cried out with fervor for all the mighty works they had witnessed, declaring, "Blessed is the King who comes in the name of the Lord! Peace in heaven and glory in the highest!"

Yet, some Pharisees, threatened by such unrestrained jubilation, urged Him to temper the enthusiasm of His disciples. His response was profound: "I tell you, if these were silent, the very stones would cry out." (Luke 19:37-40 RSV) Praise is not merely encouraged; it is essential for every man and woman. You must cultivate a steadfast resolve to praise Him, irrespective of your circumstances.

I found that during my most tumultuous seasons, my spirit remained buoyed by praise. The presence of God enveloped me; I felt as though I was cradled in divine arms, with celestial melodies resonating like trumpets echoing from above, guiding me into a heavenly sanctuary. There was a moment I can never forget, where I found myself so enveloped in His presence that all I could see was a glorious cloud that encapsulated my room. You, too, can encounter this sacred presence. His warmth is tangible, a gentle affirmation that He walks beside you. People may notice a certain glow about you, inquiring, "What is it about you?" And beneath all the surface conversation, you know—it's the unmistakable presence of God.

My yearning for His closeness deepens with each passing day. As you journey deeper into praise, you transition into true worship—a profound reverence for the Lord that leads you into a stillness, a quiet sanctuary where you can hear His voice, that gentle whisper in your spirit. His voice is often soft, a still, small sound that touches the core of your being. He communicates with the spirit of humanity, frequently manifesting through His holy Word. When God speaks, you will discern His truth—it always aligns with the promises and proclamations found within the Scriptures. Any voice that contradicts is not of Him; it belongs to the enemy, the great deceiver and the father of lies.

The adversary seeks to silence your praise, but you must resolutely cling to the assurance that God is ever with you, walking beside you, prompting your heart to soar in worship, and igniting your spirit to rise in praise.

Praise is a powerful force, a key that unlocks the shackles of despair and every form of oppression that seeks to weigh us down. It is an exaltation that elevates the spirit, lifting us to magnificent heights where possibilities abound. In the realm of our struggles, praise becomes our greatest weapon, equipping us to engage in the noble fight of faith. This is the singular battle worth our time and effort—the relentless pursuit of belief against doubt. As it is written in 1 Timothy 6:12 (KJV),

> “Fight the good fight of faith, lay hold on eternal life, whereunto thou art also called, and hast professed a good profession before many witnesses."

Here lies the essence of our courage: to grasp the life intended for us and proclaim it amidst the chaos.

Praise is not merely an expression; it is the evidence of transformation. While the unsaved may simply lounge within the four walls of a church, arms crossed, and hearts closed, the redeemed respond with a fervent, radical outpouring of joy and gratitude. Their praise flows from a wellspring of experience, undeterred by circumstances—sorrow or joy, elevation or fall—they bless the Lord at all times! I have learned this profound lesson: to find and offer praise in every situation, no matter the storms that may rage around me.

Furthermore, praise acts as a magnet for divine blessings. There are moments when God withholds His gifts until we learn to genuinely glorify Him, for praise is the key that breaks every chain. Those who wrestle with burdens and bondages find freedom when they lift their voices in adoration and worship. In these sacred acts, the grip of negativity loosens, and the enemy's hold is shattered. The devil's reign in our lives comes to an end; he can no longer impede our progress. In times of trial, it is through praise that we declare our strength. The enemy might assault us from all angles, yet our unwavering praise thwarts his sinister plots. When we engage in worship, we transcend limitations; there are no bounds for those who cherish and exalt the name of God.

Remember, your praise is not just an offering—it is your weapon in this fight of faith. Psalm 24 calls us to lift up our heads to claim our identity as victors during conflicts. Recall this scripture in your darkest hours:

> Lift up your heads, O ye gates; and be ye lift up, ye everlasting doors; and the King of glory shall come in."
>
> PSALM 24:7-10, KJV

The Lord is strong and mighty, the champion in every battle. God's Word is our sword—a divine instrument that pierces through the lies and illusions of the enemy, setting us free.

You may wonder why you remain steady while others falter around you; it is the power of His Word coursing through you. It acts as a hammer, dismantling obstacles and illuminating the path ahead. When faced with significant decisions, turn to His Word for guidance; it is a timeless compass that will never lead you astray. When faced with temptation, Jesus stood firm on His own words, declaring, "Man shall not live by bread alone, but by every word that proceeds out of the mouth of God." In combatting any adversities that arise, hurl the

Word back at the enemy, for it is sharper than any double-edged sword. In moments that require correction, the Word provides clear direction, even in the delicate task of guiding our children.

Embrace the power of praise and the Truth contained in Scripture; they will not abandon you but will uphold you amidst life's fiercest battles.

All Scripture flows from the heart of God, inspired and divine, and serves as a priceless tool for so many aspects of life—doctrine, correction, reproof, and essential instruction in righteousness. As highlighted in 2 Timothy 3:16, the sacred word must be approached with reverence, dissected carefully without distortion or alteration. This word possesses the incredible power to transform entire generations steeped in sin to liberate those held captive by their pasts. In times of spiritual hunger, God's word becomes a nourishing feast, filling our souls with satisfaction and purpose.

During my later college years, I often pondered the reasons behind my sense of isolation, questioning why I seemed to be floating on the fringes of social life. In the silence of contemplative moments, all I could cling to was the unwavering belief that my praise would serve as my refuge and strength. Every soul yearns for companionship; in the moments when friendship feels out of reach, I found solace in knowing Jesus stands ready to comfort. Scripture assures us that He sticks closer than a brother; He embraces those who find themselves alone, acting as a friend to the friendless, a father to the fatherless. He is our Comforter, the ever-present companion walking beside us through life's challenges. In our moments of turmoil and distress, He is steadfastly by our side, a calming presence amid chaos. Thank God for the gift of the Comforter.

Jesus promised that upon His departure, He would send this divine presence to remain with us always. "Nevertheless, I tell you the truth; it is expedient for you that I go away," He spoke, emphasizing the necessity of His departure for our benefit. "For if I go not away, the Comforter will not come unto you; but if I depart, I will send him unto you," as stated in John 16:7. This Comforter brings healing, freedom, and deliverance, constantly watching over us even in our moments of uncertainty. He is our strong tower amidst doubt and fear. When facing life's storms, it is enough to know that as long as we stand united with Jesus, we shall prevail. Our praise signifies courage, a declaration of standing firm in righteousness.

Praise carries us through the tumult of trials and tribulations, waging battles on our behalf lifting our spirits closer to heaven. In moments of disorientation, when the path before us seems unclear, all we need to do is lift our voices in praise to God. The scripture reminds us that all praise belongs to Him. I have witnessed God execute miraculous turnarounds in my life in the span of mere days, all sparked by an honest shout of praise. Worship holds the power to lift oppressive burdens and dissolve heavy yokes. Ultimately, it is the anointing that breaks the yoke of despair. This anointing flows from intimate prayer, a sacred communion with God. It's just you and Him—an unbroken bond where secrets can be whispered into divine ears, held closely and shared with no one else.

In His presence, I have felt my self-worth rise; God validates me, making me feel cherished and valued. I came to the realization that as long as God loves me, that truth eclipses all. I need not seek the spotlight or a platform, for in His eyes, my identity rests. I want to convey to you, dear friend, that you are important and uniquely cherished by God. When He gazes upon you, He sees His treasure, pure and priceless, an irreplaceable part of His grand design.

The sacred scripture reminds us that humanity was crafted just a shade lower than the celestial beings, a testament to the profound love and care God has for His creation. Isn't it awe-inspiring to reflect on the fact that you are among His most cherished works? Though we bear responsibilities on this earthly journey, it is through God that every seemingly insurmountable challenge can be overcome. Picture your dreams; if you can envision them, you are already on the path to becoming them. With a steadfast commitment to prayer, you will cultivate wisdom that transcends the ordinary, whether you identify as a woman or a man. In this spiritual embrace, you will experience a tranquility that defies all reasoning, as God safeguards both your heart and mind. As noted in Philippians 4:7 KJV,

> “And the peace of God, which passeth all understanding, shall keep your hearts and minds through Christ Jesus,”

you will find that divine peace envelops you, creating a sanctuary within your soul. Engaging in prayer transcends earthly existence, ushering you into a higher realm of connection with God. It serves as the essential complement to your spiritual sustenance, like butter, beautifully enriching bread, providing nourishment that nothing else can. God has endowed you with a sacred prayer language, empowering you to elevate your worship and commune with Him deeply. As you turn to Him in repentance and embrace the fullness of the Holy Spirit, a unique prayer language unfolds—a language of love and devotion waiting to be expressed. John 15:13 KJV shares a poignant reminder of love:

> "Greater love hath no man than this, that a man lay down his life for his friends."

This profound act is the cornerstone of the Gospel!

God's deep affection for you is illustrated in the incredible gift of His only Son, Jesus, who became the ultimate sacrifice so that we might be redeemed from our waywardness. The scripture tells us plainly that all have sinned and fall short of divine glory, a reminder to examine our spirits, avoid the blame game, and recognize our shared humanity. We are, at our core, sinners redeemed by grace—a grace that bestows life when we truly deserve only death and offers us protection from the clutches of darkness.

Praise and worship fortify you against any adversary; through these acts, the enemy finds himself disarmed and powerless. As you deepen your walk with God, remember this truth: when Satan tempted Adam and Eve in that fateful garden, he was cast into utter desolation. Jesus himself declared, "I saw Satan fall as lightning," as detailed in Luke 10:18, emphasizing the fallen state of evil. The adversary of your soul has been vanquished, and he cannot rise again. Embrace your identity as a warrior of Christ, a treasured child of the Living God!

Victory belongs to you—it is your inheritance because

of Christ's triumphant work on the cross. Bear in mind that He endured suffering and persecution for your sins, emerging victorious on the third day—a resurrection that assures you of His power and love. Now, seated at the right hand of God, Jesus embodies an incredible mystery: that He is God, interceding for you daily as the mediator between heaven and humanity. You have been liberated from the shackles of sin; therefore, heed the call to remain steadfast in this newfound freedom. Resist falling back into old habits or revisiting past places that lead you astray. Stay rooted in your faith community. The journey back to the shadows of sin is perilous indeed, as highlighted in Romans 6:1-2 KJV. In this divine narrative,

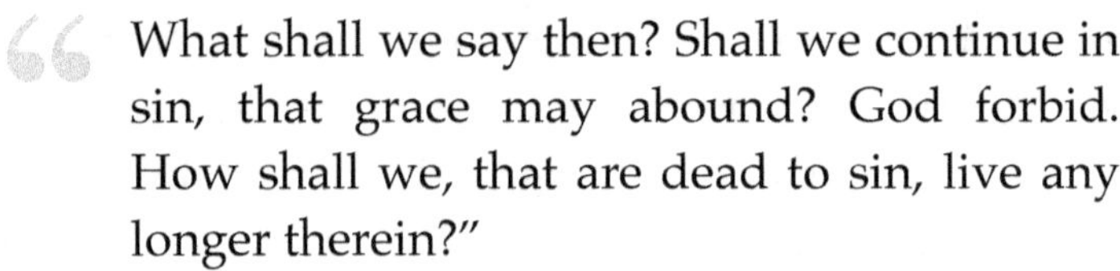

> What shall we say then? Shall we continue in sin, that grace may abound? God forbid. How shall we, that are dead to sin, live any longer therein?"

Let this be a guiding light, urging you onward in a life marked by grace, love, and unyielding faith.

Sin, oh, how insidious and treacherous it can be, leading you away from the loving embrace of your Creator, tossing you into the shadows where the light of His presence fades. Just imagine drifting away from the love that nourishes your very soul—no one desires that! It's essential, then, to remain anchored close to God. Make it your mantra always to pray and be ever vigilant about the life you lead, for it is this connection that brings unparalleled joy. Serving God is not just a task; it is a deep wellspring of happiness that fills your heart in ways the world cannot comprehend. The scriptures remind us profoundly that "the joy of the Lord is your strength," a wealth that no earthly treasure can substitute. So, seize that power and ignite that zeal within, for God desires to envelop you in the fiery passion of the Holy Spirit.

As it is written in Acts 1:8,

> "But ye shall receive power, after that the Holy Ghost is come upon you: and ye shall be witnesses unto me both in Jerusalem, and in all Judaea, and Samaria, and unto the uttermost part of the earth."

But remember, the moment you accept His Spirit into your life, it's time to rise up as a beacon of His goodness. Go forth and share the glorious news of your deliverance. When you experience something so transformative and freeing, how could you keep it to yourself? All hearts long to hear of the incredible power of God, the very force that liberates souls from the chains of addiction. He provides everything you could ever need through His Spirit. And yes, let them ridicule you as you burn bright for Him. Embracing that divine flame means you've walked through monumental struggles yet emerged unscathed—how profound is that?!

Picture this: passing through the flames without even the faintest scent of smoke upon you. What were the Hebrew boys doing in that notorious fiery furnace? They were praising God with every ounce of their being. Lean on the countless biblical examples as encouragement and worship Him even amid your chaos, for in that moment of trial, you are cultivating your faith. Consider Shadrach, Meshach, and Abednego; many labeled them as reckless for refusing to bow to the golden statue erected by the king. Yet, when that very monarch issued a decree that everyone must worship their God, the astonishment of the onlookers was palpable. You, too, may find yourself in situations that others simply do not comprehend. They might look at you, puzzled, questioning why you raise your hands in joyous surrender, but you have the intimate knowledge of all He has done and how He has rescued you from desolation time and again.

Reflect on the joyful chapters of your journey with God; those moments shine much brighter than any hardship you've faced. It's your praise that will usher you through the flames and into God's safety, a refuge where His glory is unmistakable. So, banish all complaints, for there's beauty in the lessons gained through trials—entrust them to God. He is the ultimate artisan who can weave the remnants of your struggles into a beautiful tapestry of purpose and promise, for He knows your path even better than you ever could envision. Seek His guidance daily; ask Him to lead and direct your steps. Remember, our ways are preordained by the Lord. As stated in Psalm 37:23,

> The steps of a good man are ordered by the Lord: and he delighteth in his way."

Embrace this truth, for it fuels the very essence of your journey. Embrace the joy that God has laid before you like a radiant path leading through the heart of the forest. Such joy and happiness should be the very marrow of your being!

Recently, I found myself captivated by the soulful melodies of the song "Love and Happiness" by Al Green.

While his voice is smooth, and his lyrics stir the heart, they pale against the magnificent love and happiness that God pours into your very soul. Allow His joy to permeate through every fear that grips you and every doubt that lingers in the shadows of your mind. Let Him shape your faith into an unyielding fortress of strength.

As we explore the words of James in the King James Version (KJV), we find profound wisdom nestled within the teachings meant for us. "James, a servant of God and of the Lord Jesus Christ, to the twelve tribes which are scattered abroad, greeting." Here, we gather not just as hearers but as participants in a divine conversation. "My brethren, count it all joy when ye fall into divers to see God weaving patience into the fabric of our lives. Recognize that patience is a process, an intricate dance where flaws yield triumph. "But let patience have her perfect work," urges James.

Picture this: as we embrace our challenges with joy, we are not just enduring; we are triumphantly transforming, becoming perfected in spirit, lacking in nothing. Too many succumb to defeat, failing to recognize the victories hidden within their struggles. Shift your mindset—count every moment, every tear, every setback as a step toward a glorious victory, for in them, God is crafting resilience within you.

So, when adversity knocks on your door, leap! Leap for joy! This is your season of blessing! Lift your praises high, not rooted in what you can see around you—those fleeting shadows—but in the faith that moves mountains, in the trust that guides you onward.

2 Corinthians 5:7 says,

> For we walk by faith, not by sight."

Like David, let your heart sing praises to the Lord in every season, triumph, and trial. David approached every battle cloaked in the name of Jesus—powerful, unwavering, transforming. Reflect on this: Are you invoking that same power? Some giants loom large in our lives precisely because we neglect the strength found in His name. When I proclaim "in Jesus' name," darkness flinches, and boundless power surges through me. His name bears weight; it has the ability to unlock doors that mere mortals cannot even budge. Trust in it! Let His name lead you—every step you take is a testament to His divine purpose for you on this earth. And what a purpose it is! It eclipses every fleeting concern or plan you might harbor.

Our existence is woven not merely for our earthly pleasures but to resound with His glory! Let this truth wash over you: you were created to uplift His name, to offer praise through your everyday actions.

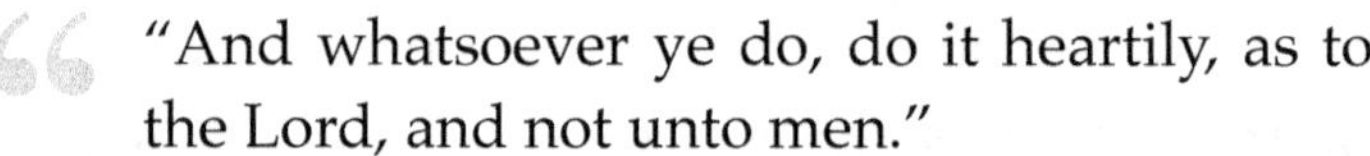

> "And whatsoever ye do, do it heartily, as to the Lord, and not unto men."
>
> COLOSSIANS 3:23

Rejoice in the season of God's breaking process; embrace it fervently! Leap for joy that you are chosen, hand-picked for divine growth and transformation! Every heartache and every challenge was orchestrated for a purpose—yes, that breakup had to happen; that divorce played its role, and those bills surfacing were designed to lead you to His glorious light. Count it all, joy! In every moment, let your heart echo praises—be assured, your transformation is part of a greater, divine symphony!

No matter what trials may surface, there is a profound truth that anchors my spirit: God is always by my side. This fundamental belief becomes my lifeline in times of despair, a reminder that His presence shadows me with unwavering support wherever I tread. He is not a mere mortal who lies or a fickle entity swayed by whims; He is steadfast in His promises, the Alpha and Omega of our faith. When chaos unfolds and life's storms rage around me, I cling to the assurance that if God permitted events to transpire, it is, by divine order, ultimately for my benefit. To truly embrace the splendor of life, a heart steeped in gratitude for one's relationship with God is essential. Even amid the dark clouds of depression, let your spirit shine through praise.

Your adoration holds immeasurable significance to Him, acting as a fragrant offering that rises to heaven like a beloved dish prepared with care for the family. Just as a lovingly cooked meal draws loved ones close, so does your praise cultivate an intimate bond with the Divine. Your heartfelt declarations have the incredible power to invoke God's intervention—a gentle yet powerful stir of His spirit on your behalf. If you yearn for His mighty works to unfold in your life, do not overlook the importance of those blessings voiced. With each utterance of gratitude, you signal your readiness for liberation.

God is poised to free you and your loved ones from the chains that bind you. He is the Author and Finisher of our story, assuring us that everything He begins, He completes. He exists in all places at all times, ever vigilant over your family, walking with you through your darkest moments. Even as troubles seem to glare from every corner, remember that the Lord your God accompanies you on this journey, an unwavering promise that transcends our understanding. It is no coincidence that you were chosen for this divine purpose; He selects the most seasoned soldiers for His great design. Your openness to His call will enable your unique role. Indeed, your praise possesses the remarkable ability to liberate others from their own prisons of despair—every chain that clings to the spirit must eventually yield.

God will never abandon His people to live in captivity. The prolonged bondage of the Israelites stemmed not from His lack of will but from their own disobedience. He seeks to guide you toward your Promised Land, but this journey requires a heart attuned to His voice—much like the respect you would show for an authority figure in your life. Just as you dedicate time and thought to those you cherish, carve out time for the Divine. He longs for connection, waiting eagerly for moments when you turn your heart toward Him. He desires the fruits of your lips—the joyful noise that expresses your gratitude and devotion.

Reflecting on all that God has graciously performed in my life leaves me overwhelmed with gratitude. He has blessed me abundantly, providing reason after reason to maintain an unyielding song of praise, regardless of obstacles that dare to intrude. In a heart full of thankfulness lies the essence of faith: an unwavering commitment to give glory to the One who sacrificed everything for my redemption. I remain steadfast in praise, joyful in my heart, and assured that this attitude will mirror the depths of His love and the vastness of His grace throughout my life.

Being thankful intertwines deeply with surrendering your heart to God. Each morning that greets you, courtesy of His divine mercy offers a unique opportunity to lay down your own will and embrace His. His plan is imbued with richer joy and profound peace—a peace that surpasses all understanding. As our Creator, when you allow Him to guide your life, you start to blossom into the person you were meant to be. Surrendering to God is not merely an act of submission; it is the ultimate expression of trust, a declaration that you're ready to make sacrifices to prioritize His divine vision over your own earthly desires.

When you choose to surrender, you relinquish all your carefully laid plans and replace them with His. Your mind, will, and emotions gradually transform into instruments of His purpose. It's a journey of metamorphosis, where God deftly shapes and molds you into the very essence of who He desires you to become. It's about letting go of the old you, paving the way for the new. This is not just about survival; it's about thriving! God stands ready to open countless doors that can lead you toward a life overflowing with abundance. A life that clings stubbornly to independence breeds heartache and suffering, shackling you from genuine praise and gratitude.

The spirit of thankfulness, however, is a powerful force—one that can elevate your relationship with God to heights you've never fathomed. It will usher you along the right path, reinforcing that gratitude and surrender go hand in hand. Avoid the trap of regret; every experience

—no matter how challenging or painful—plays a vital role in sculpting your character, preparing you for the incredible journey ahead. Those struggles you faced, harsh words that were flung your way or ill intentions cast upon you, only served to forge your strength. Shift your focus from the past pains to the bright future that awaits. You are emerging, like a caterpillar breaking free from its cocoon, transforming into a magnificent butterfly that gracefully navigates through life's colors.

Though you may not see your growth, know that others do. Their admiration—quite apart from your own awareness—counts amidst your silent metamorphosis. Allow each year to be brimming with unfathomable joy—a joy so profound it feels beyond the capacity of mere words. Just as Job experienced restoration, so shall you receive blessings double-fold for your troubles. Because you have chosen to trust in Him, He promises to supply every one of your needs abundantly. His love for you is immeasurable, underscored by the ultimate sacrifice of His only Son, granting you liberation from all that binds you. No love can ever rival the divine love of God. It seeps into the depths of your soul, igniting a spark that carries you through times of trouble when nothing else can.

Consider a mother's love; it epitomizes God's unconditional affection, standing resolute through your toughest trials. From childhood until now, I have felt her unwavering support, assuring me that everything will be alright, wrapping me in a warmth that is irreplaceable. We must cherish the praying mothers among us, particularly at this time when many choose to wander aimlessly instead of nurturing their connection with the divine. In their quest for meaning, they drift, not knowing which path to follow, lost in the absence of surrender to God. To grasp the gold that lies within God's best, you must be moldable. Never jump off the potter's wheel—let Him craft you as a striking piece of art, a vessel of His glory.

No one can treat you with the same tenderness and love as God can. He is gentle and compassionate, never imposing but always inviting us to draw closer to Him, to find solace in His perfect presence. Embrace the changes; embrace His shaping hands, for in them lies all the potential of who you are destined to be. come unto me, all ye that labor and are heavy laden, and I will give you rest. This invitation, found in Matthew 11:28-29, invites each soul weighed down by life's burdens to take refuge in a divine embrace. "Take my yoke upon you," He urges, "and learn of me; for I am meek and lowly in heart: and ye shall find rest unto your souls." In those words lie a promise as vast as the heavens—a promise that assures you, if your load feels insurmountable, you need only give it to God.

Let go, release your grasp, and trust in His infinite capacity to carry your burdens and transform every chaotic moment into the tapestry of grace. He is the omnipotent God, unmatched in power and presence. He is capable of altering any circumstance, breaking every chain, and lifting every weight from your weary shoulders. Fix your gaze upon His goodness; let your feet tread the path He lays before you. Your journey of faith, fraught with trials yet filled with triumphs, will surely be worthwhile.

As I pen these reflections, just days after my twenty-eighth birthday, I find myself overwhelmed with gratitude for the strength He has generously endowed upon me. This Christian journey has been nothing short of a magnificent adventure, where I have encountered God more intimately than I ever could have imagined. During my tumultuous moments—especially during the heart-wrenching pain of my divorce—it was His reassuring presence that guided my steps and enveloped me in love. Even now, as I write, I embark on an ongoing quest to deepen my relationship with God, a journey that continually liberates me from the chains of my past.

It is through this divine freedom that I have gained true wisdom, a maturity rooted in learning and growth. No longer do I stumble into the same snares repeatedly; instead, I stand still and wait upon the Lord, allowing His timing to unfold in my life. Being steadfast aligns with surrendering to His format—"Letting go and letting God," as is often echoed in our hallowed gatherings. The majesty of God's divinity ignites a fervor within me, compelling me to serve Him every day of my life. His goodness is undeniable; it is a call to action to try Him, to experience firsthand His sufficiency.

While the visions of angels and heavenly realms, akin to those Paul described, are splendid, nothing surpasses the understanding that His grace continuously upholds me. His loving protection shrouds me daily, guarding me against dangers seen and unseen, as His will guides each breath I take. Remember that man cannot forge his own path; it is only through yielding to God's leadership that we can reach our true potential. When you truly taste the Lord's goodness, you begin to grasp how powerful praise can be in drawing you from despair.

In trials, I have discovered that my weapon lies in gratitude. Through every tempest and tumult of life, I have remained standing strong under the mighty hand of God, for when that divine hand rests upon you, no force can deter the blessings meant for you. Embrace the joy in surrendering to His will—He seeks to uplift you, never to harm. His mission is to guide you toward life's highest satisfaction. Through every trial, through every flame, know that God walks beside you, steadfast as a friend and mighty as a warrior, ready to lead you toward an enduring peace that surpasses all understanding.

CHAPTER FIVE
EMBRACING THE JOURNEY

Every journey unfolds through a meticulous sequence of events, a systematic chain that guides us toward our destined moments. This concept of process embodies the essence of order, reminding us that our Creator, the Divine Architect of the universe, is intrinsically a God of order. As we navigate life, we are urged to let everything unfold decently and in accordance with a higher design. To find true fulfillment, one must align with this divine order; it is here that we discover the sacred roadmap of our lives.

Occasionally, we encounter those magical kairos moments—divine appointments bestowed upon us by God. These can manifest as the serendipitous way in which you met your soulmate, the unexpected opportunity that lands you an interview on a prominent television station, or even the precious, unanticipated arrival of a newborn into your family. Each of these instances is not just mere chance but carefully orchestrated occurrences that serve to mold and shape us into the likeness of God.

When I ponder the significance of the process, I imagine the structured order found in a bustling restaurant, where every chef has a distinct method of preparing exquisite dishes. The waitstaff follows a precise system for serving, ensuring that each meal arrives on the correct plate at the precisely right moment. Just as in these culinary pursuits, everything truly worth cherishing in life is intricately woven with the threads of a process. This journey isn't merely about the immediate outcome; it's about reaching the apex of achievement and fulfillment. Reflecting upon the extraordinary life of Jesus, one can see that without a sacred process guiding his path, he would not have become the extraordinary mover and shaker that he was, forever inspiring countless souls through the ages.

Consider the apostle Peter, if you will. Picture him at sea, wrestling with the waves when Jesus approached, beckoning him with the call, "Come, and I will make you fishers of men." This profound invitation marked the beginning of a divine journey, yet it was just the starting point; Peter had a path to navigate, a process through which he must travel. God had to show Peter how to walk closely with Him, step by deliberate step, day by day. It was essential for Peter to attune himself to the very life-giving words flowing from the mouth of Jesus, for one day, he would be called to transform the world in remarkable ways.

As recounted in the Book of Acts, Peter received a directive from God to linger in Jerusalem and to wait until he was endowed with power from on high. This waiting period was not a passive pause; it was part of a divine process. My friends, let us reflect together on this truth: without process, without a journey through trials and lessons, true goals remain elusive. When we embrace the process, we find that our ambitions can unfold seamlessly.

Consider for a moment the intricate ways in which God leads mankind. Every innovation, every creation that humankind has unraveled, was conceived from the very fabric of God's divine blueprint. Each one of us was crafted with purpose, each fiber of our beings woven together by the Creator for a higher calling. When we endure the trials laid before us, we emerge not just unscathed but enriched—more knowledgeable and ever more prepared to seize the challenges of the world with unwavering confidence. Endurance is, ultimately, about finishing strong.

You may find yourself feeling weak or overwhelmed at this moment, yet I encourage you to speak strength into your existence. I recall a time when I gazed into the mirror, confronting a shell of a young man—fragile and battered by life's relentless currents. In that moment of reflection, the Holy Spirit stirred within me, urging me, "Proclaim courage upon yourself every day as you face that mirror." Heeding that inner voice, I began to affirm daily the spirit of courage rising within me, and soon enough, I felt that strength take root.

Take heed: do not wait for motivation to strike before embarking on your goals. Instead, rise and tackle each task that lies ahead. If you linger for that specific feeling, you might remain trapped, unable to step out of the confines of your own bed. There were countless mornings when I lacked the desire or the fortitude to rise, yet through prayer, the Spirit of God surged within me, restoring my strength. Remember, endurance isn't defined by your present condition; it is a testament to your destined journey, illuminating where God is leading you. Each trial, each tribulation you encounter, serves only to guide you closer to Him.

So, gather your courage and understand that the process is not meant to shatter you; rather, it is designed to mold and refine your spirit. You must be pliable and willing to be shaped in the hands of the Creator. In Jeremiah 18, the Lord spoke to the prophet, instructing him to visit the potter's house. Upon arrival, he witnessed the potter skillfully shaping a lump of clay. The scripture reveals that the pot being crafted was marred in the potter's hands, yet he skillfully reshaped it into another vessel—one that seemed good and fitting to him. God questioned Jeremiah, saying, "Can I not do with you as the potter does?" Just as the clay yields to the potter, so are we to submit ourselves to His divine hands.

Here lies a fundamental truth: God employs natural illustrations to convey supernatural realities, bridging the gap between our tangible experience and divine understanding. He communicates with the limited mind of humanity, which, bound by its constraints, often struggles to grasp the vastness of existence. Yet, in this interaction, He reveals a profound purpose. Every moment you encounter is a divine orchestration, an alignment with your unique destiny. You must begin to see that everything operates in harmony for your benefit. Nothing you endure is without significance, and not a single experience goes to waste. Every fleeting second holds meaning in the grander scheme of God's plan.

Consider the very act of creation—where even God followed His own paradigm, taking six days to breathe life into the cosmos. He spoke forth the sun, the moon, and the stars, bringing them into being with deliberate intention and unwavering precision. Each element of creation was crafted with care, reflecting an exquisite order that resonates throughout the universe. Imagine a world devoid of process; chaos would reign supreme, leaving us adrift without a guiding hand. It is through this divine order that we are able to fulfill God's will, navigating our path with intention and clarity.

Thus, every trial, every joy, and every mundane occurrence contributes to a larger tapestry that signifies God's relentless presence in our journeys. In recognizing this, we can embrace the truth that even in our struggles, there resides a purpose as profound as the cosmos itself.

In this closing segment, I find it fitting to share with you the very first poems that danced from my thoughts onto the page. These creations hold a special place in my heart, acting as reflections of my early inspirations and my journey as a writer. The inaugural piece in this collection is titled "Magnificence and Royalty," and it encapsulates the splendor and grace that I aspired to capture in my youthful expressions of art. Each line echoes the dreams and ambitions of a budding poet, intertwining the lavish imagery of nobility with the raw, unfiltered emotion of discovery.

> Trust in the Lord with all your heart and lean not unto your own understanding; in all your ways acknowledge Him, and He shall direct your path.
>
> PROVERBS 3:5-6

In the stillness of a sacred dawn, I inked these words, a testament born from the depths of my soul, a time woven with threads of sincere consecration before the Lord. Amidst the shadows of a heart unraveling, struggling through the tumultuous seas of a divorce, I discovered a profound connection, a communion with the divine unlike any I had known. It was as if, during this age of sorrow, the heavens opened, and the Lord drew near, cradling my shattered heart in His gentle embrace, whispering solace into the void. For He walks alongside those burdened by grief, a quiet promise resounding through the echoes of despair. And in that sacred space, I found joy anew, a faint spark illuminating the darkness—Enjoy, for in this dance of brokenness, grace flourishes like wildflowers in a sunlit field.

MAGNIFICENCE AND ROYALTY

Magnificence and Royalty embodied;
a radiant tapestry unfolds before my eyes.
I am His regal offspring,
born from the sacred womb of grace.

In His divine embrace, I soar beyond earthly realms,
lifted up to the heavens, caressed by the clouds.
No elixirs of man can ever match
the euphoria He gifts me;
His love ignites my soul,
an exquisite high unmatched, unfathomable.

For He is my one true lover,
the heartbeat of my existence;
how wondrous this journey has just begun.
With Him amid the rain's tender kiss,
joy unfurls in every droplet,
transforming a mundane day into paradise.

The tempestuous winds howl, and the waves crash
fiercely upon me;
yet I stand unbowed, unyielding, untouched by chaos.
I revel in His presence,
where the anointing flows like a river of light,
a cascade of mercy washing over me.

O, how I tremble in reverence before Him,
my heart a canvas painted with devotion.
He is the essence of my being,
mine in totality, I declare.
I'd relinquish every treasure,
every fleeting desire for a moment
spent in His radiance, in the heartbeat of His majesty.

My soul cries for Him, my dearest friend,
for He is the Alpha and Omega,
the dawn and dusk of my life.
He was there to whisper hope into my darkness,
He is here now, a beacon of steadfast love,
and eternally, He shall remain.

Cast off the shackles of guilt,
allow His presence to wrap around you
and set you free from the chains of pain and sorrow.
He'll ignite your spirit—
an ember caught aflame,
a dance of light against the shadows.

Each hurt shall dissolve in His grace,
no need for the wisdom of the scholars
or the healing of the experts.
In this vast tapestry of existence,
though the burdens of life may press heavily upon my shoulders,
His fervent love endures like an everlasting tide,
washing over me, renewing my spirit.

The King, with His hand outstretched,
will lead you through the labyrinth of trials.
Feel His love envelop you;
this truth, sacred and unwavering,
is no mere illusion.

Place your trust in the Lord,
drawing strength from His mighty heart;
you shall emerge anew, perfumed by His eternal
embrace,
radiant as a rose in full bloom.

This is a poetic reflection born from both struggle and celebration:

SANDS OF TIME

I find myself peering up from the valley's depths,
my eyes fixed upon the lofty peaks above,
a realm of possibility glimmering on the horizon.
Armed with spiritual binoculars,
I witness the breathtaking panorama—
the very essence of contentment radiates from within.

As I sift through the sands of time,
each tiny grain embodies a memory,
a fleeting moment of existence.
With reverence, I release them into the cosmic flow,
trusting the Lord of all creation to guide my path.

The journey has not been without its trials;
quagmires of quicksand, heavy muck,
and suffocating clay have threatened to pull me under.
Yet, in those moments of sinking despair,
I gleaned clarity—I was close to feeling utterly
unworthy.
But now, I realize that even the simplest of actions
can ignite a spark of inspiration in others,
illuminating their faces with newfound hope and joy.
I take each event one at a time,
celebrating the small victories that tether me to the
divine.

As the world continues its relentless spin,
I ponder the dimming shadows of fear and strife:
lights flicker to life across Kenya,
whispers of Ebola fade, and the government stands with
resilience.
Amidst an ocean of conflicting narratives,
I resolve that—true or not—
none shall diminish the spirit within me.
The conversation about identity may swirl
like a tempest on a distant isle,
yet I proudly stand in the light of my heterosexuality.
Seeking freedom and wholeness becomes our unifying
battle cry.

Will the creation rise to partake in this divine promise,
or will they falter in the quicksand of despair?
Fear not, for blessings will soon flow,
washing away the teardrops stained upon the cheek.
We are kings and queens in the sight of God—
an iridescent tapestry woven from distinct threads:

Sonship, Hebrew, Haitian, Indian,
and all united in pride.

Will you bear witness as He returns in favor,
or will you drift unnoticed through the sands of time?
Call out—"Who's falling? Not I! Not I!"

In my sojourn, I have mingled with the community,
sharing food with the hungry—children and adults alike—
offering perishable goods and heartfelt conversations
that hoisted me from the mire.
We gathered, savoring morsels of neatly packaged bread,
sharing stories, laughter like sunlight breaking through the clouds;
truly, enough said.

There is something profound in the seemingly endless expanse
of dry sand in the Louisiana desert,
but know this: I dwell here only for a season.
I rise, uplifted, knowing we shall not linger in this state forever.
I once marched alongside determined souls,
calling for an end to violence in one of the city's most perilous neighborhoods.
As the day's light waned, I questioned those
who remained trapped in their own quicksand.
Yet, prayers are potent—a balm for our wounds.
Together, we confronted the enemy that day,
striking a blow against injustice
and uniting in pride for our shared identity.

A Black entrepreneur, philanthropist, author, and poet;
all this blossomed within a mere four years,
who could have foretold it?
Time's sands are ever-fleeting,
and so I earnestly must engage in my Father's work.

You, the vibrant generation of the future,
need not prove yourselves through fear;
rather, let us embrace the hand of God
as He gracefully lifts each grain of sand from beneath us,
elevating us all into His embrace.
The essence of time in this earthly realm is dwindling,
yet we are custodians of the sands of time.
Perform well, for in His eternal design,
time never truly ends.

Jeremiah 29:11 speaks of hope:

> For I know the plans I have for you," declares the Lord, "plans to prosper you and not to harm you, plans to give you hope and a future."

Isaiah 64:1 calls for divine intervention:

> Oh, that you would rend the heavens and come down, that the mountains would tremble before you!"

Birthed from pain, family struggles, and trials, I do not amplify the burdens I carry; instead, I exalt God, who gently steers me through life's tumultuous vicissitudes.

~

We are one, intertwined in the tapestry of existence.
At times, tears cascade, a silent outpouring from the depths of my being,
each drop, a testament to the fragility of life,
flowing through my tear ducts as a gentle reminder
of this divine creation, fragile yet resilient,
cradled in the palms of the Almighty.

In clarity, He illuminated my soul,
just as He opened the eyes of the disciples,
whispering to us: we are One.
One body harmonizing into a singular sound,
a symphony of purpose.

Remember the essence of the uno—
for in the Lord, faith, and baptism,
we find our beginnings, our unity,
an unbreakable bond.

Penning my pain, expressive ink flows
from the crevices of my heart,
and in those moments, I tread the fine line of sanity,
for loving this deeply often wears heavy upon my spirit.

And yet, through it all, He sees my worth,
calling me forth to exercise my faith,
to pinch hit in this divine drama we partake in.
In His perfect timing, nothing is mere folly;
my brothers and sisters, we are one
under the canopy of His grace.

One body, entwined in purpose,
hands and feet, multi-tethered to each other,
as if under the surgeon's precise touch,
the heart beats, remapped, to embark anew.

This is my fervent plea: strip away the excess—
Lord, I come before you on bended knee,
my hands uplifted, imploring you
to grant me the strength to stand tall.

It stings to be chosen—sometimes I feel like shattered glass,
yet I refuse to utter a complaint;
for in His design, He is masterfully crafting my existence,
shaping me in ways I cannot yet comprehend.

I need you, and you need me,
like tendons and muscles intertwined,
each supporting the other in this dance of life;
let's hustle, let's thrive.

Go UL, we chant, a joyous unison
echoing our aspirations.
Yet, I sense the coward lurking, a trembling beast,
but we, we do not sway in fear;
we rest in peace, not in strife,
offering eternal comfort despite a world of torment.

O wretched man that I am, yet I can assure you,
by a margin so vast, we shall rise together,
united in this prayer, drawn by the omnipotent power of God,

conformed to His purpose,
an everlasting saga of intergalactic glory.

No soul knows our true story but ourselves;
let Him arrange the fragments,
the jigsaw of our lives piecing together
in divine synchronicity.

No doubt lingers, my tibias anterior,
directing my steps, taking me down to the root;
do you perceive the message?
With Yeshua's grace, it cannot be overlooked—
an action verb that shall surely come to fruition,
as directly as the words I send forth.

The frontalis, unyielding, guides the skin of my brow.
Are you envisioning what transpires within this sacred body of ours?
To our Heavenly Father, in humility, we bow in gratitude.
Exhortation station—bless every nation,
for it is He who moves through me.

We are the living body of Christ—
no longer burdened by stress,
arise, O lion, let your roar shatter the silence.
Let us embrace the blessings and joy,
for we are one, unyielding and united.

"HIS TOUCH"

> For the essence of God's word, alive and profoundly active, Cuts deeper than any double-edged sword, revealing souls' concealed truths, Penetrating to the core, discerning thoughts and the inner workings of the heart.
>
> HEBREWS 4:12

His touch, His divine touch, unlike any other found,
A love that envelops me, a shield, a sacred ground.
He cloaks my spirit with favor wherever I roam,
Mercy pours from Heaven, a continuous, loving dome.

Grace like waves crashing on the shores of despair,
Supplying desires, a gentle breeze in the air.
In the face of peril, He enlightens my path,
Forewarning of the snares that might incite wrath.

When I tread upon dangers, no reason to fear,
In His presence, I stand—no need to disappear.
With authority granted, the enemy's sway is confined,
This power, so glorious, transcending mankind.

Down on my knees, with strength pouring down like rain,
I cast aside adversaries like timber felled by pain.
Eradicated doubt, obliterated dread,
In the quiet corners, only courage I've bred.

Quality of faith, not merely the quantity shown,
Some battles are insurmountable; I confront alone.
Imagine me standing on a mystical square,
Bearing my cross, a testament I share.

As for Lucifer, he's banished, his time has expired,
A flash in the night, and his malevolence is tired.
Blessings abound amidst life's tangled stress,
Lifting me from the pit—my divine finesse.

In Him, my heart has found a friend, steadfast and true,
No masquerade present. Only purity shines through.
Reflect on the sun, its strength upon hardened ground,
Trials like the sun—though painful, make us profound.

Yet, He broke the chains and sculpted a heart of flesh,
Enduring hardness as a soldier and rising refreshed.
El Shaddai stirs my spirit, awakening my quest,
No need for earthly brews; His presence is the best.

Thoughts extracted, clarity ignites my mind,
I'm free to traverse the labyrinth of life, entwined.
Each transition, a dance upon the tapestry grand,
The word speaks to my soul; each whisper a command.

I shun the world's patterns, its alluring disguise,
Preferring the warmth of His love, a fire that never dies.
On tranquil roads anew, no barricades in sight,
With a gentle nudge, He guides me through the night.

"Oh, come closer, Son," His sweet voice does beckon,
In trust, I leap forward, knowing my path is a blessing.
I relinquish my might to a force beyond compare,

Propelled like a piston, reaching heights rare and fair.

Into realms where only faith's light will persist,
His touch, oh so tender, reviving what I've missed.
No need for caffeine's rush; my soul is awake,
Nourished by His spirit, every moment I take.

Produced from the Father, the young man springs forth,
In His grace-filled embrace, I find my true worth.

9/15/2015

"In a season drenched with the tears of the weary,
when sorrow echoes in our souls,
there shall be a crescendo of joy,
rapturous and sweet,
sweeping into the heart like a golden dawn."

"There will be tears."
These words flow from the well of a long, tiring day,
a testament carved from the depths of longing.
I stand resolute in my desires,
every thought framed by the embrace of God's presence.
This poem pulses with confidence
birthed from the shelter of His love,
proclaiming boldly that His affection
remains steadfast, unwavering,
even amidst our missteps.

Can you glimpse the flicker of flames
igniting passion in my eyes?
I speak with gravity about my reverence for Him.

Tonight, as so often, I find the tears welling up
because life weaves a tapestry of challenges;
and yet, it is in this very act
that I draw nearer to His divine essence.

I may test your patience,
yet you continue to wrap me in your unwavering love.
In my moments of strength,
I grasp comfort from the thought of you,
a gentle balm soothing my racing heart.
All the times I've vented my frustrations,
hurling blame in your direction,
You still hold me tight, secure in your embrace.

I wrestle with my doubts,
yet your love remains a constant force in my life.
An angel named Joneth whispers in my ear,
a spirit of joy that dances in my shadows,
eternally inclined to remain by my side.
Thus, I cast aside fear and stress
like discarded cloaks;
I am assured in the faith I carry.

I declare my existence,
yet it is only through you that I am even in breath,
so, Your Majesty, "Let your name rise in exaltation!"
I am that I am, a vessel of purpose,
my name insignificant yet draped
in the banner of red, white, and blue.
Lafayette stands tall because of you, Sovereign!

In you, Lord, lost amid this sea of words,
I yield completely, uncertain of what tomorrow unveils,

but anchored in your strength,
this delicate cup of clay shall remain unbroken.
In your embrace, I am fortified like a steadfast wall,
a city strong and proud;
hold me together, for the fissures that appear
are the testament of my being reshaped,
molded with gentle hands, one sweet moment at a time.

You envelop me as a comforting shroud,
offering a refuge; I do not need to flee or hide.
Born anew by the Holy Spirit,
I realize it is the little foxes that gnaw away at the vine;
hence, we shall exalt Him!
I strive diligently, knowing that within me,
you meticulously outline every thread of my existence;
sin wields no power here.

Who can sever the bond of your undying love?
The King approaches!
From the dawn of creation,
you knew every sorrowful night
I would lay in your presence,
the eyes of my heart opened wide to your light.

A new philosophy unfurls for those
who receive the word of God with a heart laid open;
keep Him in the sanctuary of your soul
and on the altar of your thoughts;
for He reigns triumphant through eternity.

"Recall the ancient truths of times gone by:

> "For I am God, and there exists no other;
> I am God, and none compares to me."
>
> PSALM 46:10—

"Declaring the end from the beginning,
a whisper from ancient pathways of the not-yet-known,
proclaiming, 'My counsel shall endure,
and I shall fulfill all my purpose.'"

MY REDEEMER

O my Redeemer, the one steadfast I embrace;
you are my Lord,
the essence of my soul's desire;
I stand in gratitude,
for you have wrought a transformation within me,
reshaping this fragile being in your divine likeness;
now, I find myself whole, radiant and unbroken.

You've awakened my heart to the truth
that I am a shining gem in your gaze,
ever fearfully and wonderfully crafted;
a melody of thanks flows from my lips.
O, my Redeemer, you cradle me with tender care,
your arms wrap around me like a safe haven,
holding me with love's grip,
where danger dares not tread upon my spirit's peace.

In your embrace, you accepted me as I was,
imperfect yet cherished,
cleansing my weary soul with the balm of your word.
Here I stand, swaying with the gentle zephyr,
singing like the lark at dawn,
a tribute to your grace.

Sweet harmonies and rich melodies rise from my heart,
the pitch crafted to delight your listening ear;
listen to my cry, a war cry of triumph,
How could salvation manifest in an instant so swiftly?
No mere mortal could don the mantle of savior,
only you, my Creator, my divine companion,
who took me in a holy act,
a demonstration of love beyond measure.

As your touch ignited the spark within me,
awakening my spirit,
I felt myself soaring—unbound and free.
To you, O Lord, I lift my voice;
my heart, a precious gift, unyielding,
stand firm, for a few kind words gracefully spoken
are the foundation upon which great triumphs are built.

My Redeemer, my heart's fond passion,
I am redeemed.
With profound gratitude,
I wish to honor my Heavenly Father,
the architect of this journey,
who blessed me with the gift
of writing this work of my soul.

To my beloved mother and father,
who instilled in me the sacred ways of the Lord,
I owe my heart,
and to "Mam" and "Poppee,"
my cherished grandparents,
warmly guiding me with wisdom and love.

To my pastors, mentors,
and all those who walked beside me in my trials,
I offer my heartfelt thanks.
The path has been steep, barren at times,
yet every struggle has forged a treasure within me.
Know, dear souls, that the Lord is not finished with you yet;
His artistry unfolds slowly,
for you are a treasure in His sight,
called to be kings and priests unto Him.

He stands with you in the tempest,
your comfort in the darkness.
Cling to the promise of Proverbs 3:5-6,
for in Him, your heart will find its way:

> 5 Trust in the Lord with all thine heart;
> And lean not unto thine own understanding.
> 6 In all thy ways acknowledge him,
> And he shall direct thy paths.

~

Life's mysteries may elude our understanding, but with each passing day, we will find our way through the challenges that arise. I feel an overwhelming sense of gratitude to God for blessing me with my radiant daughter, who graced this world on September 2, 2011. From the moment she arrived, she has been a source of immense joy and light, guiding me through countless dark moments. Her existence enriches my life beyond measure, and I cherish every moment we share on this earth. I want to extend my heartfelt appreciation to those who doubted my ability to succeed. To all those who said I couldn't do it—may God bless you.

This book is not a testament meant to vindicate myself in your eyes; rather, it is crafted with purpose—aiming to transform lives and inspire change. My prayer is that every individual who opens these pages feels the profound impact of God's words and that lost souls find their way back to Him, renewed in faith and spirit. In times when my strength waned, and hope felt distant, it was my unwavering faith in God that became my sanctuary.

It was in those crucial moments that I realized that no matter the trials, He was there to lean on. Because of Him, I stand unwavering—"Standing strong"—filled with hope and determination to spread His light and love in a world that so desperately needs it. I have embraced the path of sharing my insights and wisdom through speaking engagements and appearances.

Finally, here is a selection of timeless and cherished photographs that capture the essence of my life with my beloved family.

Me and mom Judy Robertson

Myself and my wife Myrle Robertson

Myself and my daughter Irieonna Robertson

My dad Aaron Paul Robertson

Myself and my grandmother Grace Benoit

Irieonna Robertson

My younger brother U.s Marine Ryan Robertson

At Pentecostals of Youngsville worshipping

My yougest brother Jareds graduation; with dad Aaron

Preaching the gospel at age 22

I host a local Louisiana television show. It also plays live through my Facebook page

My counseling diploma

Myself

For those seeking to connect, please reach out to me at
mr.robertson1990@gmail.com.
Also, you can connect with me on Facebook at
C.A. Robertson.

www.ingramcontent.com/pod-product-compliance
Lightning Source LLC
LaVergne TN
LVHW010105170826
845678LV00012B/2257

* 9 7 9 8 8 9 6 9 1 1 2 8 9 *